YOU'RE HIRED! JOB SEARCH STRATEGIES THAT WORK

RAE A. STONEHOUSE

ISBN: 978-1-9994754-0-6

CONNECT WITH US!

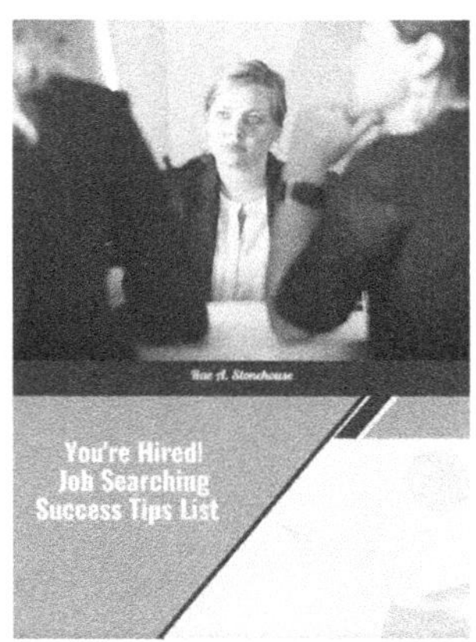

Subscribe to our **You're Hired! Job Search Strategies That Work Newsletter** to receive job searching sage advice from Rae A. Stonehouse and receive **You're Hired! Job Searching Success Tips List**, a free e-book providing you with 55 tips to landing your next job.

http://eepurl.com/ghp73f

Visit us on the web at http://yourehirednow.com.

Check out our **Jobs Now Blog** @ http//yourehirednow.com for job searching advice to frequently asked questions.

For even more job searching tips & techniques, join us on Facebook https://www.facebook.com/jobstrategiesthatwork/

This book is now available as an online self-directed learning program or an instructor-led learning program. Visit https://yourehirednow.com/online-course for more details.

CONTENTS

SECTION II

SECTION III

SECTION IV

SECTION V

SECTION VI

SECTION I

Overview & Welcome!

SECTION ONE: PART ONE

Overview & Welcome

1. OVERVIEW & WELCOME

Hi there! Welcome to **You're Hired! Job Search Strategies that Work.**

Make no mistake. Searching for work ... is work!

It takes time, effort and a lot of self-motivation to be successful in your search.

While you have your skills and experience in place to be able to apply and land your dream job, or one that leads you to it, searching for a job requires a whole different set of skills.

This book provides strategic techniques to maximize your job searching effectiveness.

Nobody can make a promise that if you follow their program, you will be guaranteed the results you are looking for and I won't either.

However, I'm confident that if you follow the strategies outlined in this book, you will be successful in landing a job.

From my experience, one of the biggest problems that job seekers often face is that they feel that they are coming from an inferior position and they don't have a lot of personal power. The belief being that the Employer has the superior position and has all the power.

Yes, they have the job and they have the power to give you the job ... or not.

What you may not realize is that many Hiring Managers are under similar pressures as you, the job seeker. They have the pressure of finding the right candidate for the vacancy they need to fill.

They are accountable to their superiors should the person they hire not work out. It has been said that an inappropriate hire can cost the organization an additional 30 to 50 percent over the job position's annual wage. This would include lost productivity incurred when the new hire is oriented, the cost of advertising for new applicants and the time taken to interview and follow up with applicants.

Hiring managers are under pressure to hire the right candidate.

Your task is become the only choice. The right choice!

As I mentioned earlier, we are likely not experts at searching for jobs and landing one. It isn't something we do on a regular basis.

As I researched the content for this book, I found that the problem is compounded by a lack of hard facts on what are the best-practices for job searching.

I'm reminded of an old parable about a group of blind men that were required to touch an elephant and to describe their observations.

Each one felt a different part, but only one part, such as a tusk or the trunk. When they compared notes, they learned that they were in complete disagreement.

I found the same to be true when researching strategic job searching skills.

Each webpage from my search results on the internet spoke from the perspective of the writer whether they were a resume writer, an Employer Hiring Manager, recruiter etc.

Much the same as the blind men describing what an elephant looks like, their advice is from their perspective. That makes sense to me. We all create our own reality. My reality is completely different than anyone else's.

The problem is that the job search 'experts' state their observations as hard facts. They believe what they write is absolutely true. And then it seems that the next article you read, will dispute what the first expert had said and they will present their truths.

How can something be both true and false at the same time? You must never do this. You must always do this.

Same advice. Can something be both yes and no?

I don't consider my self an expert at job searching.

What I am very good at though is taking subjects that people struggle with, finding better, easier ways to do things and breaking it down to basic strategies that work.

I create *systems* to solve *problems*.

Years ago, I moved my family across Canada to a city where I didn't know anyone.

I had a brand-new home built for me, but I didn't have a job waiting for me when I got there.

At the time, the new location was very hostile towards people that had moved from the east to the west coast.

I often heard "you Easterners come out here and steal our jobs..."

I found that jobs were limited. I found that getting an interview for a position I had applied for was like winning a lottery.

I also found that my new geographical area had what they called a 'Sunshine Tax.'

As it is a desirable place to live, the cost of living is higher and employers believe that they can get away with paying their employees lower wages. The idea being that you the worker should be grateful to have a job and that the employer can get away with paying you less.

'If you don't want the job, somebody else will!"

I got so tired of hearing about stealing local jobs that I started to change my story when I attended local business networking events.

Instead of saying that I was *unemployed*, I would say I had *retired* early.

I was 39 years old and the illusion I had retired early seemed to resolve the 'you Easterners' complaint.

However, I used to add 'if the right job came along, I would likely consider going back to work."

It was somewhat tongue in cheek.

It took me a good six months to land a job. It wasn't as good a job as I had hoped for.

It was definitely a compromise until something better came along.

I describe my employment experience at my new location as being like a roller coaster ride.

I went from being unemployed, to employed. I went from not getting enough hours to getting too many.

I went from being employed to being laid off.

I went from being employed to being self-employed.

Self-employment ended rapidly when I came back from a vacation to find that my only client had sold their business i.e. a vocational school and the new owners had no idea who I was or had need of my services.

Back to being unemployed.

Then I got a job in another city. It was a 90-mile round trip, daily.

I went from being at the employer's beck and call for three years working as many hours as I could as a casual staff. Then I got fired!

Then I got *unfired* and a new job, same company, a few blocks away.

I went from full time, to no time, to part time, to even more part time. Then less time and even less time.

I had to tell my manager that I couldn't afford to stay and I couldn't afford to go.

We solved the problem by me picking up hours from another worker who wanted to work less.

The downside is that I work a lot of night shifts and it is still a 90 mile, 150-kilometre round trip for work.

I think you can see why I call it a roller coaster ride.

Over the years, I have been invited to numerous job search training programs as a guest speaker, promoting the value of public speaking skills to the job search and interviewing process.

As well, I share the value of professional, business networking skills to build your business or to land a job.

THROUGHOUT THIS BOOK, I WILL BE PROVIDING YOU WITH WHAT I consider to be best practices for searching for a job.

Some of the content may disagree with what the so-called experts would say but then again... the next one would likely agree with me.

If you are a sports fan, you will recognize that any sport has a set of rules and varying degrees of competition.

Searching for a job, your job, is a competitive situation.

It could come down to two or more possible candidates, hopefully you, being one of them, having very similar credentials and qualifications.

If there was ever a time that self-promotional skills and self-confidence would come into play, it would be in the job searching and interviewing process.

Being able to effectively promote yourself can make the difference between landing the job and a 'thank you very much, but we won't be hiring you at this time."

This book is organized into Sections, covering specific topics with the content and strategies being delivered in individual Chapters.

While each Section provides specific content on a topic, it isn't necessary that you progress linearly through the book.

For example, if you needed information right now on a specific topic, you could work your way through that Section and its chapters, then go back to other ones at your own pace.

Some of the Chapters offer additional optional reading resources that can add to or help your understanding of a topic, especially where there wasn't room to expand upon the topic within the chapter. These will be featured at the end of the book under a Additional Resources Section.

In the next chapter, we will go through a quick overview of what is covered within this book.

Welcome aboard and I hope you enjoy our journey together!

2. OVERVIEW OF TOPICS & CONTENT

Here is a quick overview of the ***topics and content*** we will be covering in this book.

HERE IN **SECTION I: PART ONE** WE LOOK AT A POWERFUL STRATEGY tool called the **PDCA Model.**

We also look at the ***psychology*** of job searching and the power of ***envisioning*** your success.

In **Part Two** we dive into the topic of how to **create** and ***leverage*** your resume. Your resume is the backbone of your job search.

In **Part Three** we learn how to ***create and leverage*** your *Network Web.* Some Job Search Coaches say that this strategy alone may very well be the most effective job search technique of them all.

In **Section II** we explore how to line-up your *Cheer Leader Team.* These are your ***references*** that will help land you your job.

In **Section III** we focus on the ***initial phone call*** from the hiring department. This is the phone call that you are waiting for. The one that invites you in for an interview. Your chance to wow them!

In **Section IV** we prepare for our first job interview for a position we have applied for.

In **Part V** we look at ***four different*** personality types of job interviewers you may encounter and ***tactics*** for dealing with each of them.

In **Section VI** we dig deeply into ***common*** interview questions that you may be asked and how to make the best of your responses.

In **Section VII** we look at questions ***you*** should be asking your Interviewer, or perhaps not!

We also review job interview mistakes that ***others*** have made, so you don't make the same ones.

In **Section VIII** we focus on the follow-up phone call. This is where you phone them to find out if they have made a hiring decision and to keep your name front and center in their mind if they haven't.

In **Section IX** we focus on working with Employment Agencies and Recruiters.

In **Section X** we explore ***job searching tips*** from the Pros.

In **Section XI** we look at ***personal marketing and promotion.***

Section XII offers our ***conclusion*** and ***final comments.***

In our next chapter here in **Part One**, we introduce the PDCA Model, a powerful ***strategizing tool*** for job searching.

3. INTRODUCING THE PDCA MODEL

You may apply for a job and get hired right away. You may find that getting hired is easy.

If this is your experience, I wouldn't expect that you were reading this book.

For most of us, searching and landing a job is a challenging, if not stressful process.

The odds are that it may very well take us several attempts at applying for jobs, interviewing and waiting to see if we will get hired.

As I mentioned earlier, *searching for and landing a job* ... is a *job* in itself. And like any job, the experience you gain while doing the job is valuable.

A big part of improving in any skill is learning from your mistakes and those that others have made. Another big part of this program, is maximizing the skills that you already have and leveraging them to your advantage.

You may have noticed that I have just started calling the contents of this book a program. This book is based on an on-line e-course with the same name as this book, that I have recently published at **Live For Excellence Academy** https://yourehirednow.com/online-course. And while it is organized and written like a book, it is very much a program of strategies designed to make your job searching more effective.

At this point, I would like to introduce the **PDCA** tool.

PDCA stands for (plan-do-check-act, sometimes seen as plan-do-check-adjust) it is a repetitive, four-stage model for continuous improvement (CI) in business process management.

The **PDCA** model is also known as the Deming circle/cycle/wheel, Shewhart cycle, control circle/cycle, or plan–do–study–act (PDSA). It's quite popular in business.

You may already be using it in other aspects of your life and not be aware of it.

The first stage of the PDCA cycle is that of **Planning.** Likely, everything within this program falls in the Planning stage.

When your resume is complete, actually ... it never really is complete because you should be adapting it for every job that you apply for and your Linkedin profile has been maximized for effectiveness, you are ready to move into the **Doing** stage.

This is where you are *searching* for job vacancies, *applying* for jobs and *interviewing* for jobs.

After every step you take, you should do a ***review*** of how you did. This is the **Checking Stage.**

Did your actions taken work for you? What worked? What didn't?

This takes you to the final stage of ***adjust or acting*** .

You need to take a hard look at what *worked* and *what didn't* and make some adjustments for the next time. Then you continue with the planning stage again, making changes as you go along.

You can have one overall PDCA cycle in your mind, where you monitor the entire job searching process or you can break it down into individual areas.

How do you eat an elephant?

Answer: One bite at a time.

While I really can't imagine eating an elephant, nor would I, given the chance, the saying makes sense to me.

By breaking all the different aspects of your job search down to manageable chunks, you will likely be better able to strategize. You could create a PDCA cycle for each of the elements of your job search process.

This would likely give you a more precise view of how your strategies work.

In the next chapter, we look at an important element in job searching and that is the psychological aspects.

Your beliefs and thoughts about yourself can make a difference in your success.

4. THE PSYCHOLOGY OF JOB SEARCHING

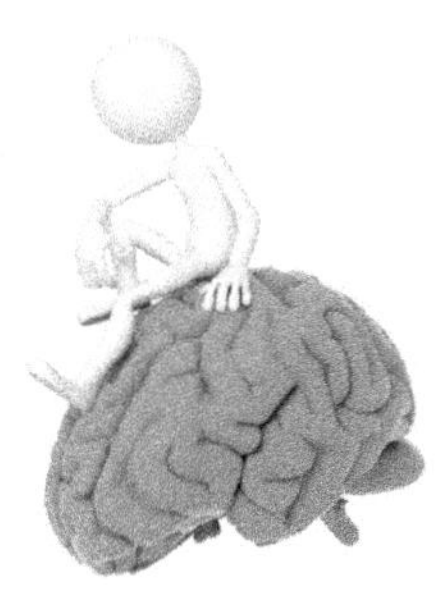

If you were to take a poll among all your friends and colleagues and asked them if they *enjoyed* looking for a job, I would be willing to bet most of them would say '*no*'.

There will always be those who enjoy any activity that involves anxiety, pressure and uncertainty. But for the most part, most of us don't. When we are uncomfortable with any activity in life, it brings out our insecurities.

Or perhaps it is the other way around? Our insecurities in life bring out our uncomfortableness with certain activities.

I made a comment in the first chapter of this section regarding our personal reality. Each of us is uniquely different.

You can't make a blanket statement saying ... 'all job search candidates have the following insecurities ...'

It wouldn't hold true.

While some people enjoy getting out there and promoting themselves at networking events, others would rather have a root canal. Some may not necessarily enjoy job interviewing but they embrace the challenge.

Others may find the process of creating and writing an effective resume to be a daunting, stressful task. And yet for others, that could be the easy part!

You can't generalize how people feel about the job searching process.

However, in my experience, there always seems to be a 'however' ... an exception to the rule if you will.

I want to direct this chapter to those of us who find the job searching process to be stressful. If this doesn't affect you, you might want to move on to the next chapter in this section.

If you do find any, or all of the steps in the job search process to be stressful, then let's take a look at how we can reduce your anxiety and make you more effective.

I'll try to break it down to common areas of anxiety and offer some possible solutions. Take a close look at any of them that apply in your situation.

As we looked at in the previous chapter, the job search process can benefit from using the PDCA process.

Over the following parts and chapters, new areas or topics will be explored.

Each step of the process will involve work on your part. It can be daunting to look forward on any task and be overwhelmed by how much work is involved.

Just remember the story of how to eat an elephant. We will be taking each step one at a time.

I've numbered the common problems job searchers have, to help organize them and to keep us focused. They are not in any order of priority or rating though.

So here are some common problems that are psychological in nature.

One: You might feel that you are under pressure to complete this program so you can start looking for a job.

You don't have to complete the program first. And actual job searching should become a daily task for you, in the sense that you devote a specific amount of time in the activity.

This program is a self-paced, so there is no pressure for you to complete it by a specific time. But of course, continuously making forward progress will work to your advantage.

Two: Many people find resume building to be a stressful process.

It's not something that we do every day. In Section One: Part Two, we break the process of resume building down into smaller steps. You can work on developing your resume, while you are working through Part Two.

It should help reduce any anxiety you are experiencing over the resume-creating process.

Three: Some people find putting their thoughts and ideas to paper, or computer, to be stressful.

Not everyone has the literacy and creative skills to create a document that reflects well on themselves. This can easily be resolved by finding a friend or colleague to help you with the process.

While they may not know the content that you want to share, after-all it is your personal story, they may be able to help you with the grammar, spelling and overall flow of your document.

Four: A common anxiety that many job-seekers experience is that they feel that they are in an inferior position when it comes to job searching.

Many don't realize the marketable skills that they have. We tend to focus on our hard skills when job searching. These are the credentials, courses, diplomas etc. that have helped us develop skills so that we are qualified to apply for specific jobs.

We also likely have a collection of transferable skills that we have developed throughout life and in our previous jobs. These don't necessarily fit into a resume but would include areas such as time management, getting along with co-workers and supervisors and being able to communicate both in a social and a professional manner.

Five: Building upon number Four, some people have low self-esteem and self-worth.

This can be a challenge in the job search process as in many other aspects of life because it prevents you from taking chances and taking advantage of opportunities.

While completing this program should help you in a small way to build your self-esteem, it is beyond the scope of the program to do so.

Of all the potential problems job seekers can face, this one has probably caused me the most challenges throughout my working life. I suffered from low self-esteem and self-confidence for the first part of my life until I decided to conquer it.

Six: I mentioned earlier that many people do not enjoy getting out there and networking.

Our anxieties seem to be compounded when we are looking for a job and need to network. We erroneously think that we are in an inferior position to another person who already has a job and perhaps that we are not worthy of getting a job.

As Sig Sigler, American sales expert and motivational speaker would say "That's stinkin thinkin!"

We have every right to be employed and we also have the right to be out there and promoting ourselves in search of that job that is right for us.

Seven: Negative Thinking. This problem likely encompasses elements from the previous six problems.

Earlier, I mentioned that job searching is very much like competitive sports. The same mind control tactics that high-performance athletes use in the pursuit of winning their competition can work in job searching.

When I say mind-control, it may bring up images of secret agents and spies and some form of torture being applied to control your mind.

Well, maybe it does for me ... I read a lot of spy novels ... and secret agents too. When I talk about mind-control, I'm referring to you, controlling your own mind.

That may sound like a no-brainer, pun intended. Of course, you are in charge of your own mind.

Who else would be? And that is the heart of the problem. Your mind believes whatever you tell it.

This goes back to the self-fulfilling prophesy or that you create your own reality belief. If you tell yourself that you will not be successful in any step of the job searching process, then well guess what? You won't be!

Self-fulfilling prophecy is in effect.

Your mind doesn't see itself as being a winner or being successful. So, it won't be!

On the other hand, does a strong positive attitude with a winning attitude guarantee success in whatever endeavour you are undertaking?

Not necessarily. Maybe not at first.

It isn't a matter of having happy, positive thoughts relating to a specific task you have completed, such as completing a job application and applying for a job. It is a daily way of thinking.

It is a way of thinking of life that becomes a habit for you.

When searching for a job and not getting the results that you want, it can become discouraging and you may even get to the point that you wonder "why bother?"

Far too many job searchers have acted upon their negative thinking and acted upon their internal "why bother" thoughts and abandoned their job search activities.

So how do we rid ourselves of *stinkin thinkin* and replace them with *positive, empowering* thoughts?

WAY BACK IN THE 1970S A SELF MIND-CONTROL MODEL OF 'SELF-affirmations' became popular.

The concept builds upon that of self-fulfilling prophecy and your mind believing what you tell it.

The idea of daily self-affirmations was developed from there.

The idea being that if you tell yourself something positive every day, your mind will get in the habit of listening to what you tell it and start to change for the positive.

When I first learned about self-affirmations, I thought it was pretty hokey.

Around the same time the television show Saturday Night Live created a reoccurring skit based on a character named Stuart Smalley. Comedian Al Franken portrayed Stuart Smalley and it became a parody of the daily self-affirmation concept.

If you do a Google search for Stuart Smalley, you will see some of his videos. They are good for a laugh.

He made popular a phrase that goes ... 'I'm good enough, I'm smart enough and Doggone it, people like me!"

As I said, at the time, I thought the concept was hokey and that the idea of saying a simple phrase to yourself every day could change your life, seemed even more ridiculous.

I read several books that helped change my mind on this subject. I found that some 70% or more of the self-talk thoughts we have on a daily basis, are negative in nature.

You *can*'t do that! You *don't* know how to that! You've *failed* every time you tried to do this.

The research further said that women are worse than men when it comes to this stinkin thinkin.

If we go back to the idea of your mind believing what you tell it, why not tell or give it something positive?

While I now believe that there is value in the 'I'm good enough, I'm smart enough" portion of Smalley's self-affirmation, I still think the "and Doggone it, people like me!" part to be a little silly.

Job searching can take time. When you are waiting for something to happen, the pressure likely increases.

I would suggest that you develop your own set of daily affirmations that have special meaning to you. Find words that are meaningful to you. Start using them regularly.

It will take time for you to start seeing results. It has been said that it can take up to 21 days of using a new skill or thought for it to become a habit.

I would suspect that in time, you will start to look at other aspects of your life in positive ways. Basing it on my own personal experience, I know that it works.

I was very cynical and pessimistic in my early years. It took a long time for me to become an optimist, while still being a realist.

I enjoy being an optimist much more than living as a doom and gloom pessimist.

In the next chapter in this part, we look at a powerful job-searching technique ... envisioning your success.

5. ENVISIONING YOUR SUCCESS

Moving forward, I want to take you in a slightly different direction.

An empowering technique that athletes use is visioning. As part of their training they imagine every step of their performance.

They view themselves as being successful and winning. Their mind believes what they input to it.

If they believe they will be successful, odds are they will be successful. There is no guarantee of course. That would be magical thinking.

I do a lot of public speaking and delivering workshops. In advance of me speaking, I will envision myself delivering my presentation to an enthusiastic audience.

'I'm good enough, I'm smart enough and Doggone it, people like me!"

When it comes to delivering presentations, your audience wants you to succeed. If they didn't, they wouldn't likely be there in your audience.

Just prior to my speaking, if I have access, I will also stand in front of the room that I will be speaking in and from where I will be speaking. I envision my audience in front of me and I see their happy smiling faces enjoying what I have to say.

For an added touch, I may envision a couple standing ovations just for fun. I haven't received the standing ovation yet, but I regularly do see the happy smiling faces in my audience.

Now how do we apply visioning to the job search process?

As you will see throughout this program, there are many steps in searching for a job.

When you apply for a job, think positive. If you don't, you're doomed for failure before you even start.

When it comes to job interviewing, this is where visioning can really pay off. If you have never been in a job interview situation before, of course it will all be new to you.

If you have, then you will recognize that an interview is composed of many steps.

The employer contacts you. You acknowledge them and set up an interview. You show up for the interview.

There are some social rituals that take place. The employer drills you with questions. You answer their questions and then you ask yours.

You leave them and go on your merry way, then you wait and wait...

As you can see, an interview can be broken down to several stages.

You can and should use visioning to act each step out in your mind, before doing it live. There is value in imagining your success in every step of the job interview process.

Doing so in advance, can help you predict any potential problems. When you are actually, doing it live, it may seem quite easy since you have already done it several times and you survived.

This is where the visioning pays off. It doesn't necessarily guarantee success but your positive, self-confident demeanour may very well make the difference of you being offered the job over another applicant.

IN THE NEXT PART, PART TWO WE DIVE INTO WHAT MIGHT BE considered the basic building block of the job searching process ... your resume.

SECTION ONE: PART TWO

Resumes: Your Ticket to Job Searching Success

1. RESUMES: YOUR TICKET TO JOB SEARCHING SUCCESS

Welcome to Part Two... Resumes: Your Ticket to Job Searching Success.

You would think that creating a resumé would be an easy task.

Even spelling it looks a little weird.

In Canada, resumé is the sole spelling given by the Canadian Oxford Dictionary; résumé is the only spelling given by the Gage Canadian Dictionary (1997 edition).

In the US & Canada, there are three major spellings of this word: résumé, resumé, and resume. And that comes from Wiktionary.

You will likely see several different spellings throughout this program.

They are all acceptable.

I would expect that if you were researching the internet for advice on how to create a resumé, you would become awfully frustrated. I know that I certainly was.

There is the old-school way of creating one and the so-called new ways to create a resumé.

The problem seems to be that nobody really agrees on what the new way is.

Everybody has their own 'pearls of wisdom' that has either worked for them or is based on their personal perspective of the job-searching process.

If you dig deep enough, you will notice patterns on the advice given. Each piece of sage advice to the positive seemingly has someone else who believes the opposite.

Much of the resumé writing advice is given in absolute positives 'you must do this!", 'you must never do this!' or 'that is so out-dated ... here is how you do it now!'

'Write for a robot resume reader' or 'don't write for a robot resume reader. That's so 2016!'

What I have tried to do is to create a system to help you create your resumé, yourself.

I've highlighted techniques and tactics gathered from self-proclaimed experts on the internet and have organized them in a manner that should make it easier for you to decide for yourself and create a winning resumé.

So, what is the purpose of a resumé?

If you're fairly new to job searching, you might have been led to believe that a resumé is the document that gets you hired.

That's not precisely how it works.

Your resumé is indeed the document you use to apply for jobs (along with a customized Cover Letter where appropriate).

However, the real function of your resumé is to simply whet the employer's appetite and get them to want to call you for an interview.

It's critical to always bear in mind that your resumé is a tool with one specific purpose: to win an interview.

Some people write a resumé as if the purpose of the document was to land a job. As a result, they end up with a really long and boring piece that makes them look like desperate job hunters.

The *objective* of your resumé is to land an interview and the interview will land you the job (hopefully!).

Your resumé is not a place to brag; nor is it a place to be modest. Its sole purpose is to generate interest in you.

What differentiates you from the competition?

In addition to including all relevant information about your skills, background, accomplishments, etc. you should find ways to include details that could generate curiosity.

If you are new to the job market, perhaps you are just out of school and haven't developed a repertoire of skills yet, you may find yourself looking for what is called an entry level job.

You may find yourself dropping your resumé off at various businesses with the hope that they may have a vacancy and your resumé might entice them to call you. In this case, your resumé becomes a 'leave behind.'

I'm reminded of a couple local young fellows who didn't quite understand the concept of 'leave behind'.

The two of them were on their way to drop off some resumés at local businesses in the hope of finding some work.

For whatever reason, they decided to do a B&E, that is a break and enter of a home, on the way to pass out their resumés.

Being very polite, when they broke into the house, they took their shoes off at the door so they wouldn't make a mess.

When they were finished with burglarizing the home, they went on their merry way, back to dropping off their resumés.

There was one big problem though.

In their haste to get away from the house, they had put their shoes on and closed the door, but one fellow inadvertently left his resumé on the floor beside where his shoes had been.

I can feel you wincing.

Yes, this is one leave behind that you never want to do. I'm pretty sure that he got an interview out, but not quite the one he had hoped for.

Who is going to read your resumé?

It depends on the job you are applying for and where it is located.

For a larger company, there may be a Hiring Manager, whose duty is to review resumés for specific job vacancies.

A smaller organization may have a manager who finds themselves having to fill two or three vacancies a year. Then there are those managers who find themselves hiring for the first time.

You also have Recruiters who are paid on commission for every successful candidate that they place into a job vacancy.

The hiring managers for large companies may use software i.e. robots, to review incoming resumés, sorting them into 'yes' for follow-up by human, or 'no' straight to the waste paper basket or Trash in cyberspeak.

You supposedly only have ***5 to 6 seconds*** to impress or catch the eye of a hiring manager who may be tasked with reading several hundred resumes for a single job.

But then again, they may only be getting a few resumes in each mail delivery.

One way or another, you need to create a resume that not only catches the attention of whoever receives them but you want them to dig deeper and contact you for an interview.

Your resume's purpose is to get you called for an interview, not to get you the job.

IN THE NEXT CHAPTER, WE LOOK AT HOW GRAMMAR, SPELLING AND formatting can help you get invited for a job interview ... or not!

2. GRAMMAR AND SPELLING/FORMATTING

It goes without saying ... avoid spelling or grammatical errors but I'll say it anyways "avoid spelling or grammatical errors!"

Yet, it may very well be one of the biggest reasons that job seekers are not called for an interview. There are some recruiters who will discount your resumé the second they see a spelling or grammatical error.

Your eyes often see what you meant to type instead of what's really there.

Although it can be painful, make sure you don't just read over your resume several times, but also that you have a friend take a peak, too.

You would be well off to locate a friend that has good grammatical skills, or you could pay someone to review your resume. It's easy to miss even big, embarrassing mistakes when you've been looking at your resumé for too long.

An objective reader can make a big difference in helping you catch spelling and grammar problems as well as many of the other mistakes identified in this section.

It is particularly important to proofread carefully if you are applying for jobs that require writing skills and/or attention to detail. For a potential future boss, your resume is your first work sample and should reflect your ability to write, edit, and proofread if hired.

Let's look at some specifics:

Watch Your Tenses

Improper tense is another common error that can really hurt you in the eyes of hiring managers.

If you are still actively working in the role you are describing, use the present tense and use words such as *manage, deliver, organize.*

If you are describing roles that you have had in the ***past***, use past-tense verbs. Some examples are 'managed, delivered, organized.'

Avoid First Person Pronouns

As a general practice, don't use words like "I" or "me" or "my."

So, instead of saying "***I*** hit and exceeded company sales quotas 100% of the time" say "Hit and exceeded sales quotas 100% of the time."

Employers look at your social media profiles to see if they can find out more about your qualifications, to see if you are creative, and to see if you'll be a good fit with their team.

They'll also be watching for red flags such as poor grammar and spelling, anti-social behaviour, or anger issues.

CONSISTENCY

Your resumé must be error-free.

That means no spelling errors, no typos. No grammar, syntax, or punctuation errors.

In addition ... there should be no errors of fact.

Any recruiter or hiring manager will tell you that such errors make it easy to weed out a resumé immediately.

You should list your information in a consistent way.

Let's take a closer look at formatting.

You want your resumé to stand out, but there is such a thing as standing out in a bad way. You may think it's creative to use 6 different fonts and colours, but that kind of creativity tends to just look clumsy.

Avoid too many font types and steer clear of font sizes that are too big or too small. Big fonts make you look like you are SHOUTING (and can also indicate that you don't have enough good content to fill a resumé with normal-size text).

Small fonts may help you keep your resumé to one page, but it's not worth it if the reader has to squint.

You should also avoid long paragraphs and long blocks of text.

Most people scan resumés very quickly and often skip over long paragraphs and miss key information.

Use white space and bullets to make your resumé format easy on the eye. Use of bullets can also ensure better reader comprehension when visually scanned.

You should leave comfortable margins on the page and make sure that everything is neatly aligned. Look neat. Look smart.

Also, keep in mind that there's a good chance your resumé will be scanned electronically as more and more companies use special software to index resumes.

If you're using wacky fonts, the software may not pick up important keywords in your resumé.

Save and send your resumé as a **PDF**, rather than a Word document, as it freezes it as an image so that you can be sure hiring managers see the same formatting as you.

If you send it any other way, there's a chance that the styling, format, font and so on, could look different on their computer than yours.

Labeling your resumé file correctly is important.

Too many people save this important document with random or generic file names like sgks123.pdf or resume.pdf.

Remember that recruiters will see the name of the file that you send them and also remember that they get tons of resumés every day. Make it super clear whose resumé they should click on by saving it under a logical name like FirstName_LastName_Resume.pdf.

I also include the date that I created the file as part of my file name. Doing so can be helpful if you have multiple versions saved of your resumé.

Even more important than naming the file in a logical manner is laying out your resume in an organized manner.

How you lay it out really depends on where you are in your career path and what you're looking to do next.

While a chronological approach is the default format, it's not always the best way to make your case.

I want to reinforce here that you need to be consistent with your formatting.

For example, if you bold the name of the organization in one section, you need to do it everywhere. Yet at the same time, be sparing with your bolding.

Your formatting should emphasize and reinforce the focus you chose, not distract from it.

. . .

As an example of consistence, every job identified on your resumé should list information in this order:

Title

Name of Employer

City and State or Province, depending on where you live and the years that you worked there.

Use **boldface**, underlining, and *italics* consistently.

If you decide to **bold** one job title, all titles should be in boldface.

If you underline one section heading, underline them all.

In addition, you should be uniform in your use of capital letters, bullets, dashes, hyphens, etc.

So, if there is a period after one set of job dates, there should be a period after all job dates.

If one degree is in bold, all degrees should be in bold.

Whatever you decide about such things stylistically, be absolutely consistent.

It may seem obvious, but spelling and grammar are critical—even if you are in computer programming or sales.

Spell check is not foolproof. Just because it's a word doesn't mean it's the word that you want to use.

A grammar error or misspelling can stand out like a sore thumb and tell the employer that you're careless. Luckily, these mistakes are easily avoidable.

In the next chapter, we look at how to feature your contact information.

3. CONTACT INFORMATION

In this chapter, we look at the correct way to use your contact information on your resume.

After all, that is the main purpose of the resume in the first place. You want them to contact you to arrange for an interview. Let's make it easy for them.

Put your name at the beginning of your resumé, with contact information on separate lines, immediately following your name.

Include mailing address, telephone number with voicemail, professional e-mail address.

Avoid slang or nicknames in your e-mail address.

Buckaroo Bonzo @ Hotmail.com might work for you if you a rodeo star but not so well in the corporate world.

A G-mail e-mail address is considered more professional than a Hotmail or Yahoo one.

Make it easier to contact you by hyperlinking your email address so that you're only one click away.

Ensure you have control of and access to all e-mail and phone numbers used. You only need to include one of each (e.g. you can use your cell phone number if you have voicemail).

Your voice mail should have a pleasant and professional welcoming message. It doesn't necessarily have to be your voice. It might be better to use your personal cell phone as a contact rather than have a family member answer for you when the big call comes.

Use between two and four lines for contact information.

You might want to make your name a few font sizes larger than other information so that it stands out.

If you've moved or changed phone numbers, make sure that your phone number, address and e-mail information is up to date.

You can include all social media profiles that are relevant to the application.

LinkedIn is the first on this list, followed by Twitter and the rest.

However, resist the temptation of including all your profiles, because while creative designers may need to include their Instagram profiles, accountants and engineers may not.

If you are going to post your social profiles, you need to ensure that they are professional in nature and up to date.

We'll talk about your social profiles in greater detail later on in the program.

In the next chapter, we will look at your Objective Statement.

4. OBJECTIVE STATEMENT: IN OR OUT?

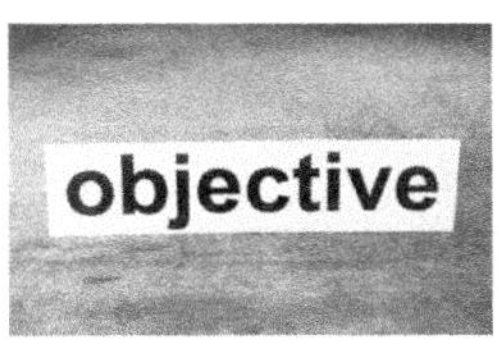

Starting your resumé off with an **Objective Statement** is one of the many 'new' rules.

Short version ... don't do it.

Why not, you might ask?

Traditionally, many resumés have begun with an opening paragraph about what the job seeker is looking for in their next role.

Employers spend very little time on their initial scan of resumés and a paragraph about your objectives contains none of the things that they are looking for.

So, this is a waste of valuable real-estate that can harm your chances.

According to the so-called experts, don't begin your resumé with an objective statement that describes your desires and career goals.

Today's hiring managers aren't concerned with what is it you're looking for—they're focused on finding the right hire. Even the most caring senior executive simply doesn't care what you are looking for – he only cares about "what's in it for me?"

He or she may care about what you want later when they know you, but for now it's all about them.

This means you need to replace the objective statement with a powerful summary that shows how you will add value to potential employers. The key is to demonstrate to the reader that there is a clear fit between your skills and their needs.

This is where the **Summary Statement** comes in or what some like to call your "written elevator speech."

We'll expand upon preparing your Summary Statements shortly.

Resumé Summary Statements

Now that we know *Objective Statements* are out and *Summary Statements* are in ... let's take a closer look at them.

Here are the Basics — Your Summary Statement should consist of a title and a few lines of text.

The text can be in paragraph form and/or use bullets. The Summary Statement should appear directly below your contact information at the top of the resumé and should reflect the general (or specific) idea of your career goals.

Starting off with ...

Your Title — This should communicate your professional identity.

Think of it as a headline that will catch the reader's eye and help them see your fit for the position at hand.

Some examples might include Social Media Brand Strategist, Senior Marketing Executive, Multifaceted Art Director and Global Operations Professional.

We talk about it elsewhere, but the title you use here in your resume's Summary Statement should be consistent with your title on your Linkedin profile.

It also means that you must customize your resumé at least slightly for each job opportunity.

Make sure that the Summary Statement is customized based on the job description if you want to catch the hiring manager's eye.

Next, we need to look at the ***Format*** — The main body of your Summary Statement should be approximately 3-4 lines of text and should NOT be written with first-person pronouns.

If you are tempted to make your Summary Statement longer to squeeze in more details, resist the temptation.

As we have said, most hiring managers spend only seconds reviewing a resumé before they make up their minds to call a candidate or not. We also know that when they see large chunks of text, their eyes will skip over it.

Therefore, it is vital to limit the length of a Summary Statement to ensure it gets read.

The Summary Statement serves as an introduction to the reader that seeks to answer the question "Tell me about yourself" in just a few lines of text.

The resume Summary Statement will help your resumé stand out by:

a. Catching the reader's attention immediately

b. Ensuring a clear understanding of your top selling points at a glance (important when hiring managers are skimming through dozens of resumés at a time and attention spans are short)

c. Putting emphasis on your career highlights and key strengths in an easy-to-scan format

d. Briefly communicating your professional objective if relevant (if the objective is not obvious)

. . .

EVERY RESUMÉ CAN BENEFIT FROM A SUMMARY STATEMENT. FOR SOME candidates, it can be critical.

Here are some specific groups of job seekers that can benefit from using Summary Statements in their resume.

1. **Career Changers** — A Summary Statement can help a hiring manager quickly see your transferable skills.

Without a Summary Statement, a recruiter might look at your most recent experience, assume you're not a fit because your experience isn't traditional and toss your resumé.

2. **Recent College Grads** — A Summary Statement can help you customize your resumé for different opportunities.

This is especially helpful if your background is somewhat general.

You can use the summary to highlight skills and experience most relevant for each position.

3. **Experienced Professionals with Diverse Backgrounds** — For experienced professionals, a Summary Statement can become the "executive summary" of your resumé, tailored for each position.

This allows you to pull the most relevant and impressive skills and career accomplishments and feature them at the top of your resumé.

NEXT, WE ARE GOING TO LOOK AT *HOW* TO WRITE YOUR RESUMÉ Summary Statements.

Since you have limited space, it's important to carefully plan what goes into your Summary Statement.

Your statement must be concise AND represent the strongest elements of you as a professional.

Here are three steps to writing a strong Summary Statement for your resumé:

Step 1: First, think of three or four skills that define you as a professional.

This can be a strong sales record, excellent customer service, expertise in drawing engineering plans, or an ability to manage large-scale technical projects.

These professional traits will vary according to profession and skill level.

Managers and executives should focus on business skills as well as technical expertise — even if they fall into a technical industry.

Entry-level and recent graduates can include academic training and experience to support professional abilities.

Step 2: Next, think of the things you enjoy the most in your work.

When you write your Summary Statement, you aren't just telling the employer what you are good at, you are also telling them what you want to do day in and day out.

Therefore, no matter how well you do something – don't talk about it if you don't want to do it.

Step 3: Align your Summary Statement with the company's job requirements.

Once you identify the skills you want to focus on, do some research and see if they line up with job requirements listed for the positions you are seeking.

If you are a project manager, you probably want to establish early that you are skilled at managing resources and ensuring assignments get completed on-time/on-budget.

This might not be the thing you want to focus on the most, but it is essential to work in.

In the next chapter, we look at examples of "written elevator speeches" or summary/branding statements with titles.

5. SUMMARY BRANDING STATEMENTS

In this chapter, we look at examples of "written elevator speeches" or summary/branding statements with titles.

Our first example is for a **PROFESSIONAL WRITER.**

A versatile and creative writer fuses a background in journalism and academics with expertise in business writing to deliver quality, customized material spanning news, marketing, web content, curriculum, and career development.

Provides sales support and highly-rated client service and excels in meeting deadlines in quick-turnaround settings.

Our second is example is for a **FINANCIAL & OPERATIONS SUPPORT PROFESSIONAL**

Blends academic training in economics and business administration with hands-on experience in sales and operations support to offer employers a track record of delivering on tasks accurately, efficiently, and quickly.

Known for providing best-in-class customer service and communications in a variety of business settings.

WHAT WE CAN SEE FROM THESE TWO EXAMPLES IS THAT THEY ARE SHORT and to the point.

There should be no confusion or misunderstanding in the mind of the Hiring Manager as to what the applicant is all about.

Here are some more helpful Tips on creating your Resumé Summary Statement.

TIP 1. CUSTOMIZE IT FOR YOUR EXPERIENCE LEVEL

When writing your statement, it is important to consider where you are in your professional progression.

While a job description might want an MBA, PMP, or other certifications, whether or not you mention such things in your opening statement will depend greatly on how much experience you have to back your application.

If you are a young job seeker and don't have a history of jobs to refer to it's okay to rely on your academic experience to strengthen your qualifications.

And it is best to call that out from the start.

Here is an example:

THIS ONE IS FOR A **BIOLOGY GRADUATE.**

Blends lab management experience with academic training at the University of Victoria to offer solid skills in clinical experiments and research activities.

Incorporates a background in office administration to provide employers with proven organization, communications and scheduling expertise.

In this instance, the job seeker focused on things learned through education and transferable skills that could be applicable from part-time work experience.

On the other hand, if you have strong experience, there is no need to rely on your academic training any longer and it doesn't need to be mentioned.

Tip 2. Focus on your most important selling points

Some requirements can be covered in the body of the resumé and just aren't important enough to place in that opening paragraph.

One example is proficiency in MS Office.

Even if you are a technical professional, software and hardware skills need their own section on the resumé and don't belong in the opening statement.

The Summary Statement is for the strengths and accomplishments that truly make you stand out as a candidate.

Of course, there are other things you might want to call to the reader's attention early, including language proficiencies, award-winning performance, or being named on one or more patents.

While these qualifications can be contained in the body of a resumé (and should still be placed there), it could be relevant to highlight them early to establish your unique value as an employee.

Tip 3. Skip the "I" and "me" stuff

Don't start your opening paragraphs with first person pronouns. An example would be "I did this ... then I did such and such."

While you do write the paragraph in present tense, you write it as if you are the understood subject of the resumé. This allows the focus to remain on the employer.

Use of "I, me, my" places the focus on the applicant and the goal of the resumé is to sell the employer on what you can do for THEM.

By telling the reader what you ***"do"*** and what you are ***"known for,"*** you get the reader thinking about how you can do those things for them.

This message should be reinforced throughout the resumé as you use achievements and certifications to reinforce your opening paragraph and highlight examples of when you have done the things that your Summary Statement promotes.

IN THE NEXT CHAPTER, WE EXPLORE THE PRACTICE OF SENDING A COVER letter with your resume. Should you, or shouldn't you? We'll see!

6. COVER LETTERS

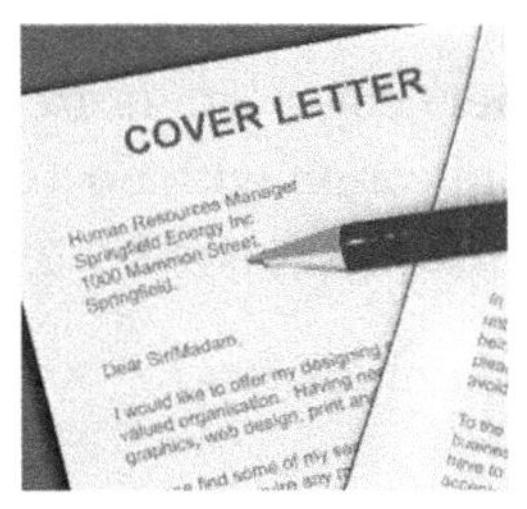

Cover letters seem to be another one in the 'are they in or out of fashion' categories.

It likely depends on who you talk to.

There seems to be a trend that many Employers don't seem to adhere to a standardized process for receiving cover letters on their corporate Websites.

Some sites have space to upload or paste in a cover letter; others do not.

Job seekers are less likely to write a "formal" cover letter when e-mailing their resumés to others.

A simple note such as ("Looking forward to speaking more about [xyz] might suffice. Or...

"My resumé is attached.") is not uncommon.

Whether it is as effective as including a more formalized cover letter, remains to be seen.

It turns out that with **Applicant Tracking Systems (ATS)** what some people call robots, often taking the first pass at screening resumes, the cover letter is often never actually read.

If a resumé contains the right keywords, it gets past the software filters and can be read by a human. If the recruiter sees the skills and experience that they are looking for, then the resumé can be short-listed for a phone call – otherwise it's passed over.

In either case, the decision was made without referring to a cover letter.

One of the most common mistakes that people make is to create a standard resumé and send it to all the job openings that they can find. Sure, it will save you time, but it will also greatly decrease the chances of landing an interview (so in reality it could even represent a waste of time).

In the **Applicant Tracking Systems** (ATS) era, where cover letters are often not read, this equals sending in a generic application with no job or employer-specific customization. Those quickly get tossed.

Tailor your resumé for each employer. The same point applies to your cover letters.

It is quite important to keep to the employer's submission requirements. Above all, you won't get noticed if you don't follow all of the specific requirements that have been instructed in the job description.

Often both resumés and cover letters are requested in a certain file format (doc, pdf, docx, rtf).

Sometimes advertisements request applications be sent or addressed in a specific way. Adhere to these, and you'll be one step ahead of any other applicants who didn't bother to tune into this detail!

Whether a cover letter is requested or not, I believe there is value in creating one, even if it just helps you clarify and wrap your head around the specific job you are applying for. You don't necessarily have to send it.

Tell what you know about the employer, its products and services, customers, industry and competition either on your resumé or cover letters; this will show the hiring manager or recruiter that you are particularly interested in their job and have done your homework.

This extra work on your part could create instant interview opportunities for you and perhaps help you answer some interview questions when you land the interview.

A Pro Tip about creating cover letters is to utilize a combination of paragraphs and bulleted lists to convey your information. And don't forget to keep your cover letter on one page, otherwise it may not be read.

In the next chapter, we look at how to leverage your work experience.

7. EXPERIENCE SECTION: SKILLS & ACCOMPLISHMENTS

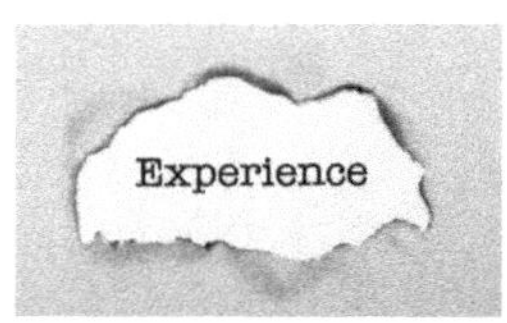

In a resume, *experience*, is another way for saying that employers are looking for positions you have held in the past.

The *'Old School'* way of completing this section would be to list all of your skills to showcase how experienced you were under each job listing.

Here is yet another example of how times have changed.

The purpose of this section is to highlight your top three to five qualifications to a potential employer, from each previous job position.

Your content needs to be crafted so that it features you as a solution to the Employer's problem.

If you include this section and you should... use a bullet format and highlight only the skills and/or qualifications that are relevant to the position you are applying for.

And substantiate with a *brief* explanation of the experience(s) that helped you build that skill or quality.

We will talk about using keywords later in this program.

Career experts recommend that you customize your resumé for *each* job, especially at the beginning of your resumé.

General or generic resumes *do not work* in today's labour market.

For some jobs, you can change a few sentences to focus on certain skills and accomplishments. For others, you may need a *completely new* resumé.

Employers value the skills that you have developed, regardless of where you developed them.

This includes skills developed in school, volunteering, extra-curricular activities and in paid employment. Since many employers use past performances to determine whether a candidate will be successful on the job or not; emphasize what you can offer potential employers (or bring to the table) drawing upon your collective experiences, skills, accomplishments, training/education and capabilities.

Validate all relevant successes and contributions made to past employers using numbers, dollars or percentages wherever possible.

Link your experience, skills and abilities to the competency requirements of the job you are applying for using examples of past successes on the job; this will enable the recruiter or hiring manager to visualize you performing the same or a similar role successfully for their organization.

It's easy for people to put any set of skills or abilities on their resumes, but unless you can show those skills in action and the results you got with them, you may not make it to the interview.

Accomplishment statements will demonstrate that you're someone who can get the job done and do it better than other applicants.

Here's another way of looking at it.

When you get to your work experience, don't just list titles and dates. Use a few lines of text to weave a story for hiring managers.

Remember a time in your previous work history when you accomplished something beyond your usual job duties.

Depending on the job and the skills you want to highlight, this 'accomplishment' could be anything between resolving an issue with an upset customer to achieving one million dollars in sales within one year.

Here's some examples:

When did you change industries? Why were you promoted? Where do you aim to go next?

The only way to make yourself look unique is to dig into what you did beyond the expected. Just remember to make it reflect one of the skills asked for in the job posting.

Then, use bullet points to back your claims with relevant facts and figures.

Statistics are an easy way to prove you did more than the job description demanded.

Many professional resumé writers use a technique called **CAR or SAR** statements.

Essentially, you're sharing a challenge/situation/problem, the action you took to address it, and what the result was. Ideally you want to frame the result by sharing how it positively impacted your employer or client.

These are the kinds of statements that make impact and tell a story but also give the reader context. Remember to keep it short; mercilessly edit it down to the least common denominator.

In resumé writing it's also a wise practice to lead with the result/impact to the client or employer because this is usually quantifiable.

Here is a quick example of what I mean by a S.A.R. statement:

Situation/Challenge/Problem: Company operated at a loss of $960,000 in 2014.

Action: Personally vetted by CEO for company turnaround. Cut costs by 30%, revamped hiring practices to reduce turnover, overhauled budget and spending practices.

Result/Impact: Delivered $650,000 profit in 2015.

You can likely use the same format as the example to write your accomplishment statements.

Also note: No bot, nor human, is looking *specifically* for soft skills.

So, delete overused phrases like "quick learner," "hard worker," and "great attitude," and sub in a list of hard skills.

Distinguishable tech and social media knowledge is particularly relevant in today's job market, and no, the Microsoft Office suite doesn't really count, unless the job posting is looking for proficiency in it.

If you're having trouble completing this section, you might have luck by looking to past performance reviews for ideas.

What have your bosses and coworkers said that you do better than anyone else?

Or, some might put it as, "What is your superpower?"

Differentiate this section from the *summary* at the top of your resume by focusing on quantifiable evidence. Think dollar signs and percentage points.

As I was writing this last section it occurred to me that the previous advice and perhaps a lot of it applies to someone who is applying for a job in the business sector.

But what about those of us working in the healthcare sector or other service industries? We may not have any access to being able to influence the financial health of the company.

I would think that removing financial references and substituting customer satisfaction, how complaints were handled and/or quantifiable results from your specific industry would be a good substitution.

This will take a little work and creativity on your part. Well, probably a lot of work.

IN THE NEXT CHAPTER, WE LOOK AT HOW TO HIGHLIGHT YOUR education.

8. EDUCATION

In this chapter, we look at how to showcase your education and a few other miscellaneous items worth mentioning.

List your education in reverse chronological order – degrees or licenses first, followed by certificates and advanced training. Set degrees apart so they are easily seen.

Put in **boldface** whatever will be most impressive.

Include advanced training, but be selective with the information, summarizing the information and including only what will be impressive for the reader.

No degree yet? If you are working on an uncompleted degree, include the degree and afterwards, in parentheses, the expected date of completion: B.S. (expected 20__).

If you didn't finish college, start with a phrase describing the field studied, then the school, then the dates (the fact that there was no degree may be missed).

You might want to use a different heading on your resume rather than Education.

Other headings might be "Education and Training," "Education and Licenses," "Legal Education / Undergraduate Education" (for attorneys).

Awards

If the only awards you have received were in school, put these under the Education section.

Mention *what* the award was for if you can or just "for outstanding accomplishment" or "outstanding performance". If you *have* received awards, this section is almost a must.

If you have received commendations or praise from some very senior source, you could call this section, "Awards and Commendations." In that case, go ahead and quote the source.

Professional Affiliations

Include only those that are current, relevant and impressive. Include leadership roles if appropriate.

This is a good section for communicating your status as a member of a minority targeted for special consideration by employers, or for showing your membership in an association that would enhance your appeal as a prospective employee.

This section can be combined with "Civic / Community Leadership" as "Professional and Community Memberships."

Languages

Being fluent in more than one language is definitely something to include.

Civic / Community Leadership

This is good section to include if the leadership roles or accomplishments you have taken on are related to the job target and can show skills acquired.

For example, a loan officer hoping to become a financial investment counsellor who was Financial Manager of a community organization charged with investing its funds.

Any Board of Directors membership or "chairmanship" would be good to include.

Be careful with political affiliations, as they could be a plus or minus with an employer or company.

Publications

Include only if published and provide links where you can if you think the work is impressive and relevant. Summarize if there are many.

Comments from Supervisors, Clients, other Professional Elite

Include them only if they are very exceptional. Heavily edit for key phrases.

Personal Interests

Tread thoughtfully here. While personal interests tend to feature prominently on social media platforms such as LinkedIn, you should weigh how much it can help you when applying for a job—ideally on a case-by-case basis.

It you include a section like this, keep the following in mind:

Advantages: Personal interests can indicate a skill or area of knowledge that is related to the goal, such as photography for someone in public relations, or carpentry and wood-working for someone in construction management.

This section can show well-roundedness, good physical health, or knowledge of a subject related to the goal. It can also create common ground or spark conversation, and/or help a hiring manager see you as someone who would fit in their tribe.

Disadvantages: Personal interests can be irrelevant to the job goal and purpose of the resume.

Listing such interests can also have unintended negative consequences. For example, if you're highly athletic and the people interviewing you aren't physically fit – or perhaps even self-conscious about it– the fact that you're super-fit might not play in your favour.

If in doubt, do not include a Personal Interests section.

Your reason for including it is most likely that you want to tell them about you. But, as you know, this is an ad. You are advertising yourself.

If this section would move the employer to understand why you would be the best candidate, include it; otherwise, forget about it.

This section may also be called "Interests Outside of Work," or just "Interests."

IN THE NEXT CHAPTER, WE LOOK AT HOW TO USE KEYWORDS TO GET your resume noticed.

9. USING KEYWORDS IN YOUR RESUMÉ

Using keywords in your resumé is similar to using keywords when creating a website or writing a blog. The purpose there is to make it easy for the search engines to index it and post the results. With your resume, keywords will help position you as a possible applicant for further attention.

Employers ***do not*** read every word on each resumé.

Keywords describe skills and qualifications. You might see them in the job posting that you are answering and on related companies' websites. It would be useful to carefully scan the job posting to see if any keywords pop out for you. Then you can enhance your resumé by using as many keywords as you can.

But, do not make up experiences, just to use keywords.

IN THE NEXT CHAPTER, WE LOOK AT HOW TO MARKET YOUR transferable skills.

10. MARKETING YOUR TRANSFERABLE SKILLS

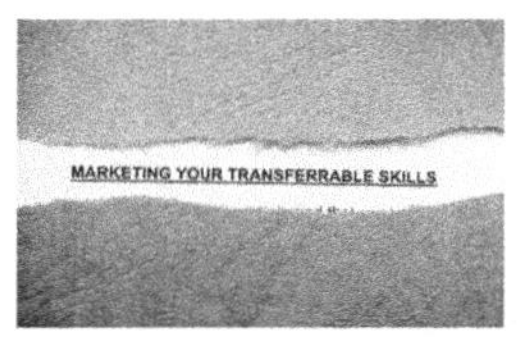

Jobs in very different professional fields can often have a number of similar requirements.

Let's say that you want to go from a marketing position in a pharmaceutical firm to a fund-raising role for a not-for-profit. What are the skills you've already demonstrated that are applicable?

They may be more than you think.

Consider these possibilities:

- Time management
- Project management
- Collaboration
- Persuasive communicating
- Strong decision-making
- Innovative problem-solving
- Composure under pressure

Brainstorm a list of skills that you have developed from different jobs that you have had in the past and see if any of them are transferable to the job you are applying for now.

In the next chapter, we look at using ***action words*** to maximize your resume's content.

11. USING ACTION-ORIENTED WORDS

Closely tied to your use of correct grammar and formatting is the use of action-oriented words rather than passive ones.

But what are they?

Action verbs are basically verbs that will get noticed more easily and that will clearly communicate what your experience or achievements were.

Action verbs *imply* that you *actively* got things done. Examples include *managed*, *coached*, *enforced* and *planned*.

Look at everything you've written in your resume and add action verbs wherever possible. If you are reworking an existing resume, change any passive words to active language.

Here is a list of what some might call Power Words.

POWER WORDS

accelerated accomplished achieved acquired addressed adminis-

tered advanced advised advocated aligned allocated amplified analyzed answered appeared applied appointed appraised approved arbitrated arranged assembled assessed assigned assisted assumed assured attained audited authored authorized awarded

blocked boosted bought briefed broadened brought budgeted built

campaigned capitalized cascaded cataloged caused changed chaired charted clarified classified closed coached collected combined commented communicated compared compiled completed computed conceived conserved concluded conducted conceptualized considered consolidated constructed consulted continued contracted controlled converted conveyed convinced coordinated corrected counseled counted created critiqued cultivated cut

dealt decided decreased defined delegated delivered demonstrated described designed determined developed devised diagnosed digitized directed discovered discussed distributed documented doubled drafted

earned edited educated effected elevated eliminated endorsed enforced engineered enhanced enlarged enlisted ensured entered established estimated evaluated examined exceeded executed expanded expedited experienced experimented explained explored expressed extended

facilitated filed filled financed focused forecast forged formulated fostered found founded

gained gathered generated graded granted guided

halved handled headed up helped hired

identified illustrated implemented improved incorporated increased indexed initiated influenced informed innovated inspected inspired installed instituted instructed insured inte-

grated interpreted interviewed introduced invented invested investigated involved issued itemized

joined

kept

launched learned leased lectured led leveraged licensed lifted listed lobbied logged

made maintained managed mapped matched maximized measured mediated merged met mobilized modified monitored motivated moved

named navigated negotiated

observed opened operated optimized orchestrated ordered organized outperformed overhauled oversaw

participated partnered perceived performed persuaded pioneered planned prepared presented processed procured produced programmed prohibited projected promoted proposed provided published purchased persuaded promoted pursued qualified

qualified quantified questioned

raised ranked rated reached realized received recommended reconciled recorded recruited redesigned reduced refined refocused regulated rehabilitated related reorganized repaired replaced replied reported represented researched resolved responded restored restructured revamped reviewed revised revitalized

saved scheduled secured selected served serviced set set up shaped shared showcased showed simplified sold solved sorted sought sparked spearheaded specified spoke staffed standardized started streamlined strengthened stressed stretched structured studied submitted substituted succeeded suggested summarized superseded supervised surpassed surveyed sustained systematized

tackled targeted taught terminated tested took toured traced tracked traded trained transferred transcribed transformed translated transported traveled treated trimmed tripled turned tutored

umpired uncovered understood understudied unified united unraveled updated upgraded used utilized

verbalized verified visited

waged weighed widened won worked wrote

yielded

12. REFERENCES INTRODUCTION

This is another one of those areas of the job searching process that have been modernized.

Where it was once appropriate to write 'references available upon request', it is now considered to be bad form. For one thing, you are stating the obvious. Of course, they are!

Asking and checking out your references is part of the hiring process should you be successful in your interview. Even more of a no-no is providing your references names and contact info as part of your resume.

If the employer has access to your references, they may just contact them before talking to you. That in turn prevents you from giving your contacts a heads up to tell them that a potential employer may be contacting them to learn more about you. You want your references to be ready to act as a cheerleader on your behalf.

We explore some reference strategies in greater detail in Section Four.

~

In the next chapter, we introduce the idea of branding your resume.

13. BRANDING YOUR RESUMÉ

I'm a strong proponent of personal marketing and promotion, blowing your own horn, so to speak. I believe that business professionals should market themselves in a professional way.

Where businesses have branded their products and services for years, this practice has carried over to personal branding. Some would tell you that this is the way to go when job searching to ensure you stand out from all the other applicants.

I'm not going to tell you that this is the definite way to go, but I will give you some info on the topic and you can decide for yourself.

One suggestion might be to create a *so-called* normal resumé as well as a branded one. You could try using each of them and see what happens.

To start with, develop a personal branding or value proposition statement and use it on your resumé, cover letters, interviews, networking and all job-related communications, including social networking activities.

When it comes to personal branding, all branding for that matter, it is important that you are consistent in all areas.

A personal branding statement or value proposition is similar to what is often called a USP (Universal Sales Proposition) in the business world. It is a short tagline that encapsulates how you *differentiate* yourself from others.

This can take some time to develop and you will want to test it on friends and colleagues to see if it works for you. You don't want to come across as being cheesy or boastful.

Please locate and read the ***Developing your USP*** document. It's available in the Resources section at the end of this book.

We talked earlier about how *Career Objective Statements* are a thing of the past. Some resumé writers believe that the strategy of using a profile summary or *career summary* is now also history.

Instead, they suggest it should include a ***personal-brand snapshot***.

The idea is that you give the reader *newsworthy information* in *short, effective statements* so they can get the facts and move on.

This reason is *exactly* why newspapers and news articles start with a great headline, give the most critical facts/details first, and then gradually fill in the not-so-critical details further down in the story. They know you want the important information first and don't want to wait for it.

Those same resumé writers advise doing the same in your resumé.

Start with your branding statement and make it answer the decision maker's questions:

"Why should I care?" or

"What's in it for me?"

When time is of the essence, answering these questions first gives readers exactly what they need to know up front; then they can choose to keep on reading for any details.

Corporate branding marketers utilize certain colours to emphasize their brand. The same applies to developing your personal brand. Certain colours may have specific meanings to ***you*** and can be used to develop your personal brand!

With ever-decreasing attention spans, some resumé writers are suggesting writing tweet-sized resumé sentences as a sound strategy. And this doesn't seem to be a trend that is fading away in the coming years either.

The next time you write a sentence for your resumé, see how many characters are included. And then see if you can get it down to 140 characters or fewer without losing impact.

Consider what is ***essential*** and what is ***critical.***

Ditch the ***essential*** and run with the ***critical.***

We go into greater detail about personal branding in Section XI where we talk about Personal Marketing & Promotion.

In the next chapter, we look at leveraging your digital media footprint.

14. LEVERAGING YOUR DIGITAL FOOTPRINT/USING SOCIAL MEDIA

Resumés, used to function as your "first impression" to an employer.

In some industries, things are *rapidly changing*. They are now *quickly becoming* the second or third thing an employer may see about you.

With the rise of social media sites such as Linkedin, website resumés, portfolios, video resumés, and job-search strategies that allow job seekers to tap into the hidden job market and bypass sending a resumé as a first introduction, the human eye is quickly becoming the #1 gatekeeper.

Employers may be *looking* for you, or someone like you, to fill a vacancy, using the very same social media tools, such as Facebook, Twitter and blogs. If you are on-line and you have your keywords highlighted to resonate with those that an employer would be looking for, there is a good chance that you will be discovered.

This is even before the employer has seen your resume.

First impressions are important - if you don't want a potential employer to see something, don't make it publicly accessible or put it online at all.

Let's look at *leveraging* your on-line presence, often called your digital footprint. You can use social media to your advantage. Remember that you're marketing yourself.

Owning your digital footprint is also about taking advantage of an additional opportunity to make a good impression. Here lays the challenge. Not everybody is on-line.

Staying off the grid on social media can work against you. While you may want to keep your private and professional lives separate, having such high privacy settings that no one can find you online, or being offline altogether, can hurt your chances during a job search.

93% of employers say that they screen candidates on social media before hiring them and *if* they can't find any mention of you online, it's a red flag. They could very well interpret it as you have something to hide – or that you're simply not very technologically savvy and not using the latest communication tools.

So, assuming, that you are on-line, how do you leverage your on-line presence?

One way is to utilize your social profiles in a way that will confirm what employers want to see. The most common websites for recruiters to screen candidates on are LinkedIn, Twitter and Facebook. What you post and how you behave on these sites can create a first impression of the sort of person you might be or want to be seen as.

Employers look at your profiles to see if they can find out more about your qualifications, to see if you are creative and to see if you'll be a good fit with their team. They'll also be watching for red flags such as poor grammar and spelling, anti-social behaviour, or anger issues.

This doesn't mean linking potential employers to your Facebook photo albums so your prospective new boss can see how fun you are when you go on vacation or having a good time at a party.

This means linking your LinkedIn profile (and if you don't have one yet, you should get one--the basic version is free) to your resumé, and making sure they match.

When Linkedin first came on the scene, it was very much like having your resumé on steroids.

Now, it is very similar to the new way that we are using for resumé writing. You don't want to just copy and paste your resumé on your Linkedin profile.

However, you should spend some time updating it so that your Linkedin profile generally contains the same job history and responsibilities as your resumé does. They should work together to promote you as an ideal job candidate.

Your Linkedin profile allows you to expand a little upon some of the details that you used in your resumé. Linkedin can also be a good venue for posting testimonials from people you have worked within the past.

Be sure to ask people to provide recommendations for you, in particular those people who can speak to the strengths that you most want to be emphasized. These aren't the same as references, however some of the glowing testimonials may very well serve as a source of references for you.

Be sure any e-mail addresses and social media handles shared are appropriate, that is ... they aren't unprofessional looking. If you have identified in your resume publications or articles that you have written, your Linkedin profile can be a great place to highlight them.

Don't forget that you should also have a recent photo on your Linkedin profile and while it can be candid, it should also have an air of professionalism about it.

Besides Linkedin, other social media venues offer valuable possibilities for powering your job search, as well as a few potential downsides. Be sure your digital footprint is an asset as you prepare your resumé.

Make sure you own your digital footprint.

Social media is a primarily a vehicle for communication. You will want to include at least one of your social media accounts on your resumé. As I mentioned earlier, be sure that any e-mail addresses and social media profile names look and sound professional. If not, create new ones.

Understand that most employers – 65% or more – use social networks to research candidates. Roughly half of them do so to see if the candidate is likely to be a "good fit" for their culture – in other words, right for their tribe.

It is documented that employers regularly review social media to see if there are reasons ***not*** to hire an applicant. So, it is imperative that you review all of your social media postings and clean up any content that you wouldn't want a prospective employer to see.

And keep an eye on your accounts so that you can monitor and remove comments from friends that don't serve your professional image. Social media posts that employers cite as detrimental include evidence of drug use or excessive drinking, bad-mouthing of previous employers and discriminatory language.

Being active on social media can advance your professional interests and possibilities. Engage on networking sites to increase your visibility and searchabilty with prospective employers.

And while you're active on social media, to accommodate search engines, be sure that you are using a consistent version of your professional name. If you're "Robert A. Jones" on Linkedin, you should be Robert A. Jones in your resume and on your other social media accounts – not Rob Jones here and there. Your professional "screen name" is probably your most important keyword especially for search engine generated results.

Let's look at using social media and on-line resources for job searching.

You can find lots of valuable information on-line about a potential employer, if you are willing to spend some time researching.

And you should!

As mentioned, follow your prospective employer on Linkedin, Twitter, Facebook, Instagram, and any other social media platform they may use. Don't forget their company website! Think of what you see as an aggregated news feed about the employer.

It doesn't take long to begin to get a real sense of the organization's culture, values, and work environment intel that can help you prepare the most thoughtful resume possible – and it can also help you immensely as you later prepare for an interview.

Make sure that you have cleaned up your own social media profile, if necessary.

What is their history?

What do they emphasize in their messaging?

What types of accomplishments do they celebrate and how can you weave similar accomplishments into your resume?

What kind of language do they use to describe achievements?

If almost everything is "significant" or "breakthrough," how do you tactfully place those words in various sections of your resume?

Who are the decision makers?

What is their hiring philosophy?

What kind of work culture is it?

In addition to digging around online and in social media, use your networking skills to learn all you can to help you customize your resume.

Do all the research you can, from on-line searches and social media tracking to networking with people you know. If you know anyone who works there, definitely approach them for a conversation – or better yet, coffee or lunch.

Research shows that your resumé must demonstrate that you have at least 70% of a job's requirements to have a legitimate hope of landing an interview. And bear in mind that one of the advantages of social media is that you can gain access to people you otherwise might not.

Search for someone within your connections who is connected to a person of interest to you. Perhaps they are in the field in which you are seeking work; perhaps they work for a company you wish to get in to – then ask your contact to introduce you.

We go into greater detail about this form of connecting in Part Three on developing your network web.

You can leverage your research results to tweak your skills and accomplishments section of your resume. When customizing your resumé for a specific position, take careful note of the skills required and use any number of those words in your resume.

If you think of yourself as someone who "leads stakeholder communications," but the employer uses the phrase "stakeholder engagement" – that's right, you're now an expert in stakeholder engagement.

If you have "increased website and social media traffic" in your current job, but your prospective employer's website discusses "online presence" – your resumé should note that you "elevated online presence."

The big caveat of course, is that you really do have those skills.

OUR NEXT CHAPTER IS SPECIFIC TO PROFESSIONALS WHO HAVE BEEN using a curriculum vitae to search for a job.

15. CV TO RESUMÉ

A Curriculum Vitae (CV) is mainly for professors, teachers, lawyers, scientists and related professionals. At least in North America it is. I understand that the term CV is used interchangeably with that of resume in other parts of the world.

This chapter is directed at professionals that use a Curriculum Vitae, which is basically a story of the professional life.

Academics may have 10- or 12-page-long CVs, or even more.

The downside with so much information is that *often*, some of their most impressive experiences get lost on page six or seven. You need to get to the point! It is recommended that you highlight your most notable achievements on one page.

The goal is to get a hiring manager to get excited about you and what you bring to the table. If the manager likes what they see, they of course can then read through your entire CV.

So, short version, change your CV to a résumé.

Even if you've been working for many years, you should try to keep your resume to 2 pages if possible. And don't throw out that CV. Some job postings may ask for either. Be prepared!

IN THE NEXT PART, WE LEARN HOW TO CREATE YOUR NETWORK WEB.

SECTION ONE: PART THREE

Introduction to Your Network Web

1. INTRODUCTION TO YOUR NETWORK WEB

Welcome to Part Three Job Searching – Creating & Leveraging Your Network Web

In this Part, we look at how to create and use your ***Network Web*** to help search for your job.

We will also look at some strategies to help you when you are out there networking. I call them *power networking* strategies.

But before we do so, it is probably a good idea to explain what a Network Web is and why you should create one.

In the not too distant past there was a principal identified as *Six Degrees of Separation*.

According to Wikipedia ... Six degrees of separation is the idea that all living things and everything else in the world are six or fewer steps away from each other so that a chain of "a friend of a friend" statements can be made to connect any two people in a maximum of six steps.

It was originally set out by Frigyes Karinthy in 1929. Karinthy was apparently a Hungarian Author.

With the rapid development of on-line social media venues, it has been said that the degrees of separation that connect you to almost anybody in the world is now down to three degrees.

If you are on Linkedin, and you should be, you can easily see that as your number of 1st degree connections increase, your 2nd and 3rd degree connections increase exponentially. Your 3rd degree connections could easily be in the millions. Linkedin used to tell you how many 1st, 2nd and 3rd degree connections you had, but they have dropped that feature.

So how do we take advantage of this worldwide interconnectedness?

The answer to that question while it is an easy one, does take some work.

The *Network Web* is a tool that helps you draw upon your personal network to find the ideal job that you are looking for. Your ideal job may not be posted yet, in fact, it may not even be created yet. Your Network Web can help put you in front of decision makers and key people that are in the position to hire you.

STEP ONE IS TO MAKE A LIST OF YOUR PERSONAL CATEGORIES.

These are your interests and the organizations, formal and informal that you belong to.

These may include hobbies, family, church, professional organizations, sports teams, current and past employment.

Create a page for each of the above categories as well as any others that you can think of.

Once you have completed the task please go to the next step in this strategy.

Step Two is to make a list of people you know in each category, start with a list of 10 names for each organization or interest category and then add 10 more if possible.

Don't worry about considering if you have seen them recently or not.

At this point, your task is to generate as many names as you can.

When you have completed this task please go to the next step in this strategy.

Step Three: For illustrative purposes, we will use this drawing. It is basically a web with you at the centre and four circles located on the web.

YOU SHOULD CREATE A DOCUMENT WITH THE NAMES OF THE CIRCLES AS your headings.

First Circle: The ***Crisis Circle*** is closest to the centre of the Web.

These are the people you can really count on.

You should have at least four people who will be supportive in the event of death, illness, divorce or bankruptcy. They can include family, friends, your doctor or lawyer.

The Second Circle: This is your ***buddy circle.***

Friends you have fun with, the people who accept you for who you are. There should be at least three people in this circle.

The Third Circle: This is your ***professional circle.***

People who you know professionally, can provide reference letters and can speak about the quality of your work and character. You need at least 12 people in this category.

The Fourth Circle: This is your ***casual friends*** circle.

People you can share ideas with. You may work with them or know them through organizations or volunteer work. Some may become closer friends and eventually form part of the more inner and intimate circles.

NOW YOU HAVE SOME WORK TO DO.

Create a list of people under the four circle's headings e.g. My Crisis Circle ... My Buddies Circle ...

Up to this point we haven't factored in our Linkedin connections.

Likely, many of your Linkedin connections will fit into your Third Circle, your *professional circle*.

Once you have gone though your Linkedin connections, go through your other social media accounts and your e-mail address book and write down names.

You'll be surprised at how quickly the list grows.

In the next chapter, we learn how to leverage the connections you have just identified.

2. LEVERAGING YOUR CONNECTIONS

In this chapter, we delve deeper into networking and how we can *leverage* our connections as a powerful job searching strategy.

You may think that you don't know anyone who can help you with your job search. But you know more people than you think, and there's a very good chance that at least a few of these people know someone who can give you career advice or point you to a job opening.

You'll never know if you don't ask!

Some Job Search Coaches will tell you that leveraging your network is the most effective strategy you can use to find your ideal job.

The **Network Web** is a powerful tool. You'll be amazed at all the contacts you do have, and can identify the gaps in the network.

With your goal of finding suitable employment in mind, you can ask:

- Who do I need to know?
- Who do I need to bring into my circle?

- And who do I know that can introduce them to me?

Reach out to your network

All the connections in the world won't help you find a job if no one knows about your situation.

Once you've drawn up your list, start making contact with the people in your network. Let them know that you're looking for a job.

Be specific about what kind of work you're looking for and ask them if they have any information or know anyone in a relevant field.

Don't assume that certain people won't be able to help. You may be surprised by who they know.

Figure out what you *want* before you start networking

Networking is most effective when you have specific employer targets and career goals. It's hard to get leads with a generic "Let me know if you hear of anything" request.

You may think that you'll have better job luck if you leave yourself open to all the possibilities, but the reality is this "openness" creates a black hole that sucks all of the networking potential out of the connection.

A ***generic*** networking request for a job is worse than no request at all, because you can lose that networking contact and opportunity.

Asking for ***specific*** information, leads, or an interview is much more focused and easier for the networking source.

If you're having trouble focusing your job search, you can turn to close friends and family members for help, but avoid contacting more distant people in your network until you've set clear goals.

Start with your references

When you are looking for a job, start with your references.

Your best references—the people who like you and can endorse your abilities, track record, and character—are *major networking hubs*. Contact each one of your references to network about your possibilities and affirm their agreement to be your reference.

We discuss strategies for working with your references in greater detail in Section Two but here are a few quick points.

- Describe your goals and seek their assistance.
- Keep them informed on your job search progress.
- Prepare them for any calls from potential employers.
- Let them know what happened and thank them for their help regardless of the outcome.

If you're nervous about making contact—either because you're uncomfortable asking for favours or embarrassed about your employment situation—try to keep the following things in mind:

It feels good to help others. Most people will gladly assist you if they can. People like to give advice and be recognized for their expertise. Almost everyone knows what it's like to be out of work or looking for a job. They'll sympathize with your situation.

Unemployment can be isolating and stressful. By connecting with others, you're sure to get some much-needed encouragement, fellowship, and moral support. Reconnecting with the people in your network can be fun—even if you have an agenda.

The more this feels like a chore the more tedious and anxiety-ridden the process will be.

Focus on building relationships

Networking is a give-and-take process that involves making connections, sharing information, and asking questions. It's a way of relating to others, not a *technique* for getting a job or a favour.

You don't have to hand out your business cards on street corners, cold call everyone on your contact list, or work a room of strangers. All you have to do is reach out.

Be authentic. In any job search or networking situation, being you—the real you—should be your goal. Hiding who you are or suppressing your true interests and goals will only hurt you in the long run.

Pursuing what you want and not what you think others will like, will always be more fulfilling and ultimately more successful.

Be considerate. If you're reconnecting with an old friend or colleague, take the time to get through the catching-up phase before you blurt out your need. On the other hand, if this person is a busy professional you don't know well, be respectful of his or her time and come straight out with your request.

Ask for *advice*, not a job. Don't ask for a job, a request comes with a lot of pressure.

You want your contacts to become allies in your job search, not make them feel ambushed, so ask for information or insight instead. If they're able to hire you or refer you to someone who can, they will.

If not, you haven't put them in the uncomfortable position of turning you down or telling you they can't help. Be specific in your request.

Before you go off and reconnect with everyone you've ever known, get your act together and do a little homework. Be prepared to articulate *what* you're looking for:

- Is it a reference?
- An insider's take on the industry?
- A referral?
- An introduction to someone in the field?

Also make sure to provide an update on your qualifications and recent professional experience.

Slow down and enjoy the job networking process

The best race car drivers are masters of slowing down.

They know that the fastest way around the track is by slowing down going into the turns, so they can accelerate sooner as they're heading into the straightaway.

As you're networking, keep this "Slow in, fast out" racing mantra in mind. Effective networking is not something that should be rushed.

This doesn't mean you shouldn't try to be efficient and focused, but hurried, *emergency* networking is not conducive to building relationships for mutual support and benefit.

When you network, you should slow down, be present, and try to enjoy the process. This will speed up your chances for success in the job-hunting race.

Just because you have an agenda doesn't mean you can't enjoy reconnecting.

Don't be a hit-and-run networker

Don't be a hit-and-run networker: connecting, getting what you want, and then disappearing, never to be heard from until the next time you need something.

Invest in your network by following up and providing feedback to those who were kind enough to offer their help. Thank them for their referral and assistance. Let them know whether you got the interview or the job. Or use the opportunity to report on the lack of success or the need for additional help.

Evaluate the quality of your network

If your networking efforts don't seem to be going anywhere, you may need to evaluate the quality of your network. Take some time to think about your network's strengths, weaknesses and opportunities.

Without such an evaluation, there is little chance your network will adapt to your needs and your future goals. You may not notice how bound you are to history, or how certain connections are holding you back. And you may miss opportunities to branch out and forge new ties that will help you move forward.

Taking inventory of your network and where it is lacking is time well spent. If you feel your network is out of date, then it's time to upgrade! Your mere awareness of your needs will help you connect you with new and more relevant contacts and networks.

Take advantage of both "strong" and "weak" ties

Everyone has both "strong" and "weak" ties.

Strong ties occupy that inner circle and weak ties are less established. Adding people to networks is time consuming, especially strong ties. It requires an investment of time and energy to have multiple "best friends." Trying to stay in touch with new acquaintances is just as challenging. But adding new "weak tie" members gives your network vitality and even more cognitive flexibility—the ability to consider new ideas and options.

New relationships invigorate the network by providing a connection to new networks, viewpoints, and opportunities.

In the next chapter, we explore tips for strengthening your job search network.

3. TIPS FOR STRENGTHENING YOUR JOB SEARCH NETWORK

Tap into your strong ties. Your strong ties will logically and trustingly lead to new weak ties that build a stronger network.

Use your existing network to add members and reconnect with people. Start by engaging the people in your trusted inner circle to help you fill in the gaps in your network.

Think about where you want to go. Your network should reflect where you're going, not just where you've been. Adding people to your network who reflect issues, jobs, industries, and areas of interest is essential.

If you are a new graduate or a career changer, join the professional associations that represent your desired career path. Attending conferences, reading journals, and keeping up with the lingo of your desired field can prepare you for where you want to go.

Make the process of connecting a priority. Make connecting a habit—part of your lifestyle. Connecting is just as important as your exercise routine. It breathes life into you and gives you confidence.

Find out how your network is doing in this environment, what steps they are taking, and how you can help. As you connect, the world will feel smaller and a small world is much easier to manage.

Take the time to maintain your network

Maintaining your job-search network is just as important as building it.

Accumulating new contacts can be beneficial, but only if you have the time to nurture the relationships. Avoid the irrational impulse to meet as many new people as possible.

The key is quality, rather than quantity. Focus on cultivating and maintaining your existing network. You're sure to discover an incredible array of information, knowledge, expertise, and opportunities.

Schedule time with your key contacts

List the people who are crucial to your network—people you know who can and have been very important to you. Invariably, there will be some you have lost touch with.

Reconnect and then schedule a regular meeting or phone call. You don't need a reason to get in touch. It will always make you feel good and provide you with an insight or two.

Prioritize the rest of your contacts

Keep a running list of people you need to reconnect with. People whose view of the world you value. People you'd like to get to know better or whose company you enjoy.

Prioritize these contacts and then schedule time into your regular routine so you can make your way down the list.

Take notes on the people in your network

Collecting cards and filing them is a start. But maintaining your contacts, new and old, requires updates. Add notes about their families, their jobs, their interests, and their needs.

Unless you have a photographic memory, you won't remember all of this information unless you write it down. Put these updates and notes on the back of their business cards or input them into your contact database.

Find ways to reciprocate

Always remember that successful networking is a *two-way* street. Your ultimate goal is to cultivate mutually beneficial relationships.

That means giving as well as receiving.

Send a thank-you note, ask them about their family, email an article you think they might be interested in, and check in periodically to see how they're doing. By nurturing the relationship through your job search and beyond, you'll establish a strong network of people you can count on for ideas, advice, feedback, and support.

In the next few chapters we look closer at some strategies to maximize our effectiveness when out there networking ... person to person.

4. DRESS FOR SUCCESS

Most of us have likely been told from a very early age "You shouldn't judge a book by its cover."

Yet we do it every day, often in the first few seconds of having met someone.

We automatically determine whether they are a danger to us, whether we would want to have a conversation with them, whether we would want them as a mate ... or to mate with.

We do it automatically.

It's part of being human and our judgement is often made with the clothing the person is wearing as one of our decision-making criteria. Being dressed inappropriately for a given situation can set you apart so that people do not want to approach you to converse.

If you are shy, having somebody come up to you to talk can be a lot easier than having to make the approach yourself. So, don't reduce your chances by dressing wrong.

Wrong? What does that mean?

There is a lot of room for interpretation. What is wrong for one person is right for another. Many people like to express themselves through colourful clothing or cutting-edge fashion.

Many people don't have a clue when it comes to dressing for the occasion.

I once attended a black- tie gala awards event. I was in a tuxedo as was my colleague. We observed some men in their cleanest blue jeans with a black string tie.

I think they missed the point.

My suggestion would be that if you were attending a business networking event, then "business casual" would be appropriate. This can become even more casual in hot climates.

If everyone is wearing shorts and you are in your tuxedo, you may get attention but perhaps not the kind that you wanted.

As for dressing for success, it has been proven over and over that most people feel better about themselves when they're dressed up. You need every advantage that you can get when you are out there networking, marketing yourself.

Don't shut the door in your face before it is even opened. People do judge others by their clothing, don't let them judge you without talking to you first.

In our next chapter, we look at business card presentation and etiquette.

5. BUSINESS CARD PRESENTATION & ETIQUETTE

In an earlier chapter in this section, we made mention a couple times about using business cards in your networking activities.

Now we are going to take a closer look at business card presentation and etiquette. If you are planning on doing some serious networking, you should have business cards available to present to another.

Not having a card to present may be a missed opportunity for you.

Besides serving as an introduction for you, they will serve as a visual prompt to remind the other person that they met and spoke to you.

It can be difficult to think of using business cards when you are searching for work and you aren't in business. It might help to think of them as being 'calling' cards.

Their purpose is to provide your name and contact information for anyone who might want to get in contact with you.

Hopefully, to tell you about a job lead.

Having business cards printed used to be fairly expensive, but now, they are within everyone's reach. Companies like Vistaprint have regular specials where you can order on-line 500 business cards for $10.00.

I have purchased from Vistaprint when they have offered special deals. 500 cards for $10.00 ... it's hard to beat that deal.

Some job-searching networkers struggle with the fact that they don't have a business to promote and they're not sure what to put on their card as their title. I believe that they tend to overthink this part of the process.

If you have a professional designation, you would insert it, right after your name. A quick example would be using myself ... Rae A. Stonehouse R.N., if I actually was looking for a nursing position.

With business cards being so inexpensive and if you are searching for work in more than one field, you could easily purchase additional cards that identify you as working in those fields.

When in a networking interaction, if you have your different cards with you, you could easily produce one that connects you with a specific field of discussion.

Now that you have your business or calling card, we need to look at the process of sharing your card. Despite what some people think, there is a protocol.

The Japanese take the presentation of a business card in a one to one networking situation far more serious than we do. To them, ritual is involved.

When presented with a business card you are expected to accept it with both hands, hold it in front of you and read the content of the card, both sides. You would then hold it with respect as the other person shares their elevator pitch.

You would only place it in your pocket after you had left the person and you would never deface the card by writing on it.

In North America, we are a little less respectful.

Sometimes, quite a bit!

I have met a fellow that within the first seconds of meeting him he announces "Well let's get this out of the way" and hands me his card. I expect that he wasn't as comfortable or skilled at networking as he thought that he was.

I have also seen an influential woman walk up to a group of people and start passing out her business cards. "Here you go, one for you and one for you!"

She then left the group and went over to another and repeated the process. It was like she was feeding chickens or passing out candy to children who were trick or treating at her door.

The purpose of passing out her business card seemed to be missed. I wonder if she was actually shy and was covering up her uncomfortableness?

So, what is the correct way to present your card to another? How and when?

I'm sure everybody has their own view on the matter.

When I have been offered another's business card as part of an introduction that is under way, I will adopt what I described earlier as the Japanese method.

I will accept it, quickly read the details and I will keep it in my hand in full view. I see the offering of a business card from another as the cue to offer mine in return.

I often make a comment about a detail or an aspect of their business card to reinforce that I have taken a serious look at it. If I don't see any action from my partner towards offering their business card, I will initiate it myself.

Asking, "Do you have a business card?" can be easier than saying "Here is my business card."

Of course, their providing a card opens it up for me to provide mine. I will also listen for a verbal cue of "I should get in contact with you", "I will keep in touch" or anything close to that as a signal for me to offer my card.

~

In our next chapter, we look at shaking hands, a necessary part of networking.

6. WHOLE LOTTA SHAKING GOING ON

I've titled this chapter **Whole Lotta Shaking Going On**, because when you are out there networking, meeting new people and greeting people you already know, there *really* is a lot of hand shaking going on.

A handshake is more than just a greeting. It is also a message about your personality and confidence level.

In business, a handshake is an important tool in making the right first impression. The same applies when you are job searching.

Your ***business*** is finding yourself a job.

Let's take a closer look at the simple act of shaking another's hand. Maybe, it's not so simple after all!

Before extending your hand, introduce yourself. Extending your hand should be part of an introduction, not a replacement for using your voice.

This isn't the cue to start reciting your elevator pitch though.

Extending your hand without saying anything may make you appear nervous or overly aggressive. On one hand (pun intended!) it would seem that shaking someone's hand should be an easy process. We have likely been doing it most of our adult life.

On the other hand, some people seem to have problems with it.

I believe that part of the problem that creates anxiety is that we over think things sometimes. We are anxious because we give more importance to the activity than it really deserves and it takes on a life of its own, creating anxiety.

A self-fulfilling prophesy if there ever was one.

Another part that likely creates anxiety is that we can only control our portion of the interaction. If our partner is an experienced hand-shaker, then all should go smoothly but many aren't.

There are a few *different* hand-shaking styles that come up in the literature and I am sure you have likely experienced them yourselves.

I personally don't like grasping someone's hand who has the so-called "**wet fish**" handshake. It can leave you with an obsessive urge to wipe your hand as soon as you can, but fight the urge.

Even worse, there are times that my hand is sweating and I don't want the label. I have developed the habit of giving my hand a quick, unobtrusive wipe on my pant leg before offering my hand.

THEN THERE IS "**BONE-CRUSHER BILL.**" THE OFFERED HAND OFTEN comes in as curve from the hip of Bill with the express purpose of crushing walnuts.

Or so it would seem.

Bill never seems to realize the pain that he causes in others or the fact that people start to avoid him. Word can get around!

ANOTHER INEFFECTIVE HANDSHAKE I CALL THE "ROYAL" HANDSHAKE.

Someone only offers you the tips of their fingers and no matter how you try you can't seem to grasp more than a few fingers. You are left feeling that you were robbed.

The bottom line is that *you* should avoid being any of these profiles. If you need to practice at home before going to a networking session, do so.

It seems to be coming more common that friends are hugging when meeting in a social setting. There are many people that are what I call "huggy" people.

I would suggest waiting to see if you offered one rather than expecting one. It could make for an awkward situation if you were to offer a hug on a first contact and it wasn't welcomed.

Maintaining Eye Contact

Closely related to hand-shaking and interacting with a new contact is that of maintaining your eye contact.

Many people have challenges maintaining eye contact with their conversational partner at the best of times. This can have different reasons.

For some cultures, it is inappropriate to look another in the eyes. Avoiding eye contact can be a sign of respect or deference to the other.

For the most part, maintaining eye contact in a conversation can demonstrate confidence. A couple challenges come to mind though.

A difference in height between the speakers can be challenging, probably more for the shorter person looking up than the taller person looking down.

Another challenge in a busy room is to focus on your conversational partner, not on people passing by or other conversations going on. It can distract you and give the impression that you are looking for a better conversation to join. If you partner is displaying this particular behaviour they may well be scanning the room for a better opportunity.

In our next chapter, we explore the importance of following up with what you said you were going to do.

7. FOLLOW-UP IS EVERYTHING!

It can be a great feeling when coming home from a networking event and looking at the stack of business cards you have collected. You even spoke at length to many of the card-donators.

Some, it can be a little difficult to recall who they actually were.

"Now was he the tall fellow with the bad hair piece .... or was he ...?" You've probably experienced that scenario more than once. And you know what ... perhaps some of the business people that you gave your precious business card to are thinking something similar.

Hopefully not about your bad hair though.

For effective business networking, I recommend the *quality* over *quantity* method of networking.

Some would say that networking is a numbers game, the *more* that you meet the *higher* the chances of your meeting someone that can benefit you.

Take for example that you are meeting someone for the first time and if the setting and conditions permit, they deliver their elevator pitch and you return with yours. Then comes the awkward moment, what to say next.

You can either carry on conversing about something of no consequence "Nice day, eh?" until one of you tires of it or you can explore common interests. Assuming, that you have a common interest, I would suggest that you take the lead in the conversation in getting the other to expand upon the commonality or something that they had previously said.

Many networkers make the mistake of trying to sell their *product or themselves* at this juncture. Your *goal* should be to arrange to meet them at *another* time, perhaps for coffee, to discuss those common areas further.

Even though many of us are electronically connected to our offices by our smart phones and can likely check to see if we are available at a certain date and time to make a coffee date, we likely won't.

When you suggest meeting for coffee, later, if the person is willing to set up a date and time, on the spot, I would go with it. Location can always be determined later by e-mail.

If they aren't willing to set a time and date, I would refer to their business card and say something to the effect of "Can I reach you at this e-mail?

"I'll contact you next week and see if we can set up a time to get together for a quick coffee."

Unfortunately, for many networkers, this is as far as they go. They don't do the follow-up. Life gets busy, there is always one more thing to do with your business and before you know it you have lost the window of opportunity.

There is a strong possibility that the individual that you were networking with also has a list of people they are following up with and other commitments. It is far too easy to get left by the wayside if you don't take action to stand out from the others.

At a recent morning meeting of my Business Referral Group we discussed the issue of follow up.

A fellow member, related that in his experience, if you actually follow-up with a lead, it puts you way ahead of those that don't.

He makes a practice of following up with a networking connection within three days of the original meeting and says that it is amazing how many people have said to him "You know, you are one of the few that actually follows up."

Yes, following up can help you stand out from the competition.

THE COFFEE GET-TOGETHER IS THE OPPORTUNITY FOR EACH OF YOU TO share your business or professional details and determine if there is enough reason to continue at another time to develop your relationship further and ideally to do business together.

You might ask "I've contacted them three times by e-mail and even left a couple voice mails but they haven't gotten back to me. What do I do next?"

There could be a legitimate reason for them not getting back to you. Life happens! But they could be acting non-assertively and are actively avoiding you.

I would have to respond with "If that was *true*, is that someone that you *really* want to network with or to do business with?" If you are to continue it could easily label you as a stalker.

One suggestion may be to add them to your tickler file. A tickler file is like a day-timer or a planner and you add a date and a time to follow up on a specific item.

A couple weeks down the road, ignoring the fact that they haven't acknowledged you yet, you would be justified in sending them a message something like "I just noticed that we didn't get together a few weeks ago like we said we would.

Where did the time go? It seems to be picking up speed.

Last time we met we were discussing our common interests of ...Are you still interested in getting together?"

If you still don't receive a response, I would put them in the "inactive" file.

When it comes to networking, to *stand out* from your competition, remember to follow-up.

In the next chapter, we look at some things that you ***shouldn't*** do when you are networking.

8. TOP 15 NETWORKING NO-NOS

Throughout this section and in articles I have written, I have provided tips & techniques to help improve networking effectiveness.

I thought it would be informative and perhaps entertaining to look at the subject from a *different* perspective i.e. what you really ***shouldn't*** do.

It's a good way to reinforce what you ***should*** do.

THESE AREN'T PROVIDED IN ANY ORDER OF PRIORITY.

See if you recognize any of them from your adventures in networking land.

- **No Show: (Not showing up for an appointment)** When all is said and done it can be argued that all you really own in life is your reputation.

There are some people that don't respect other people's time. They make appointments that they don't intend to keep, or they pre-empt the appointment for something that is more important than meeting with you.

Soon they get the reputation of not being reliable or keeping commitments. Is this the reputation that you want to develop?

- **No Follow-up: (Not following up on something that you said that you would do)**

BNI (Business Network International) founder Dr. Ivan Misner promotes the concept of "givers gain."

Offering to help someone with something or providing information that can help an individual move their business forward without expecting compensation, is a good way to develop a network connection.

Not following-up on what you said you were going to do takes away from your credibility and your reputation.

- **No Follow-up: (Not following through with contacting a connection)**

If you say that you are going to follow-up with someone ... do so.

If you don't ... at the least, you have missed an opportunity to develop a potential profitable connection. At the worst, well who knows!

See **Follow-up is Everything!** In the Resource Section for an expanded version of why you should follow-up.

- **Not focusing on your conversation partner i.e. looking around the room for a better offer.**

I think that we are all guilty of this at one time or another. Let's face it, not everybody is all that interesting to listen to.

And you know what ... our conversation partner might be thinking the same thing about us!

Listening is a skill.

You will find that the more you listen to people, the more that they think you are interested in them, the more that they will reveal about themselves and they will think that you are a fantastic conversationalist.

- **Using sexist or racist language.**

I hear this far too often in conversations with people that should know better. It isn't acceptable and I don't want to hear it.

When you are looking for work and out there making connections, you really don't want people to remember you as a sexist or racist.

- **Fly undone!**

Gents for heaven's sake check your fly when you leave the restroom.

It might be a great conversation starter "So the bull's ready to get out is it?" But is this where you want the conversation to go?

It can be challenging to recover from a position of embarrassment. Trust me I know. I was on stage for two hours once as an emcee with my fly undone.

- **I'm so wonderful! (Going on and on about yourself and not giving the other person a chance to talk)**

If you have been on the receiving end of listening to one of these types, you will know that it is not fun.

I would suggest hitting the *Pause* button and move on to the next opportunity.

While you should have your own story ready to share, which

includes the fact you are searching for work, you should be prepared to listen closely to the other person and learn more about them.

- **Talking about someone else i.e. a third party who isn't part of the conversation in a derogatory manner.**

Some people are happiest when they are putting somebody else down.

If you participate with someone like this, you are validating their behaviour and you will likely soon be labelled the same way. This is basically gossip.

You can bet, that if a gossip is telling you something juicy about someone else, they are also telling someone else about you.

Don't be a gossip!

- **Dump job: (Using your conversational partner as a sounding board without asking their permission to do so)**

We all have challenges in life, problems that are bothering us right now. It won't help your networking success rate if you become known as a whiner. That's what counsellors are for.

Leave your complaints at home and come prepared with a success-focused story to share. You don't even have to be the hero in your story. You can tell a story about how you helped someone else become successful.

- **Monopolizing the Other Person's Time:**

This is a little different than what is outlined in #7 I'm so Wonderful!

If you are shy or uncomfortable with networking, it can be easy to stay with one person longer than you should. You are depriving both of you the opportunity to meet other people.

- **Disrespecting a Business Card:**

People tend to take their business card quite seriously. It is an extension of who they are.

We aren't as serious about it as say the Japanese however, picking your teeth with someone's business card is a not a great way to make friends and influence people.

- **Hit & Run: (Acting like a Shark)**

Sharks are a type of networker that go to a business networking event with the intent of making a sale right there, right now.

They don't care about you or your business. They are only interested in what they can get from you.

Don't be one! And don't allow yourself to be attacked by one either!

- **Not having Your Own Business Cards:**

This portrays the image that you are not a serious networker.

If you haven't even taken the time to develop and produce business cards to promote yourself, then why would I want to do business with you?

I have heard it said "Oh I don't do business cards." "I take the time to write their name down on a piece of paper with their contact information."

"It's more personal, and then I contact them with hey remember me?"

"Lame, lame, lame." That's all I can say about that comment.

I recall a speed-networking event that I organized. It was very much like speed dating, except it was for the purpose of developing business connections.

One young fellow who worked as a high-end office furniture salesman didn't bring any business cards. When I asked him why he didn't bring any cards, he smiled and said "How can anybody forget this beautiful face?"

Well, I guess they did forget his beautiful face because a month or so later I saw him in his new line of work filling ice cream cones at our local Dairy Queen.

- **Eating Food While Conversing:**

Many networking events offer food & beverage.

Balancing a paper plate in one hand and a drink in the other can be challenging when reaching your hand out to shake another's hand. My personal belief is that if I am eating, I will stand to the side and chow down, then when finished, I will resume networking.

I have had to stand an awfully long time with a plate of food in my hand, while listening to another to avoid appearing rude.

Word to the wise ... be careful of spinach dips. Spinach stuck to your teeth can take your conversational partner's focus in different directions than what you intended.

- **Networking While Inebriated:**

You are your own liquor control board. If you can't handle your liquor without getting mouthy, don't drink!

What you say and do may come back to haunt you.

In the next chapter, we take another look at using LinkedIn as a job searching tool.

9. LINKEDIN REVISITED

In the last section, we briefly mentioned utilizing Linkedin as a tool to develop connections that can hopefully be a source of employment leads for you.

In an earlier chapter it was mentioned several times that your Linkedin profile should resonate with your resume.

So how do you do that?

Let's go back to basics to answer that question.

When Linkedin was first developed, we were encouraged to upload our resumes to our Linkedin profile. If you had a long work career, your experience section that included the duties and responsibilities that you had taken on over the years, could be quite lengthy.

It was very much like having your resume on steroids. It seemed the more you had posted, the better.

The same applied to creating your resume. The more you had written, the better off you were.

As they say ... the times are changing.

If you are brand new to the concept of Linkedin, let me keep it brief by saying that you can easily sign up for an account for free.

As I understand, people go to Linkedin for three main purposes:

- One, to look for *work* or *opportunities*.
- Two, to find someone to *hire* for their business.
- And three, they are looking for a *solution* to a problem they have.

When setting up your professional profile you need to be thinking *self-promotion*.

At this point in your life ... that is being in job-search mode, you need to be *easily* seen as a solution to somebody's problem. Your solution of course is that you are willing to work for them and you have the skills and expertise to do so.

The promotional copy that you add to your Linkedin profile has to not only *grab* your reader's attention from the beginning, it has to *quickly* position you as someone who is worth digging deeper into your profile.

As I have said before, your Linkedin profile, starting with your name, title and summary, should be consistent with what you have written in your resume.

Your ***Summary Statement*** from your resume fits in quite well as the summary for your Linkedin profile.

The content that you have added to the *Experience* section of your resume also fits in well to your ***Linkedin Experience*** section with the added benefit of being able to expand upon your personal information that you weren't able to do within the limitations of a resume.

If you have any publications or examples of work that you have created that would be of benefit to your job search, Linkedin is a good place to feature them.

In a previous chapter, we talked about using business cards in networking. Especially when job searching, there is value in posting your Linkedin url to your business card.

The same applies with posting your Linkedin url to your resume. You want to make it as easy as possible for people to research you and what solution you might have to offer them.

The other sections of your Linkedin profile should also be completed with a *self-promotional* slant, keeping in mind that you still need to be professional.

Back in Part Two we talked about creating the content for your resume in a self-promotional manner.

You can likely use the same content from your resume to complete your Linkedin profile, with the added benefit of being able to expand upon it.

Linkedin is not Facebook. Anything that you post to the Timeline should be professional in nature and shed you in good light. That is, it should position you as a *credible*, *experienced* if not expert, person in your field.

Up to this point, we have been talking about you promoting yourself on Linkedin as part of your overall job-searching strategy. Another equally beneficial feature of Linkedin is that you can search for jobs in the geographical area that you want to work in by entering your search query into the Search box on your home page.

Please keep professional

In the graphic below, I clicked on the Jobs link, then I entered the term 'Nurse Jobs in the screen that came up.

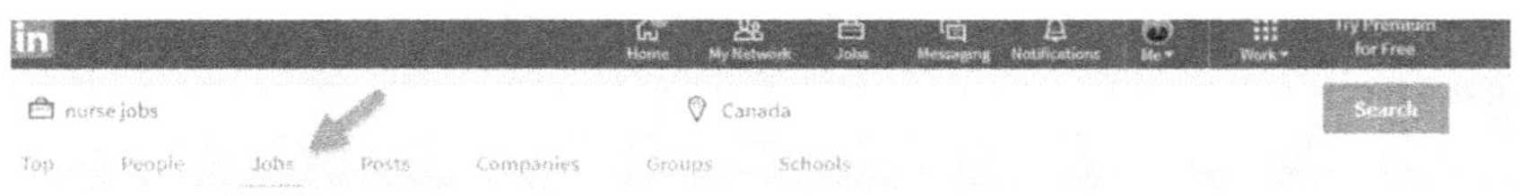

You can fine tune it for different geographical areas if you are considering relocating or your own area if you aren't.

Something to remember though is that these are just the jobs that have been listed on Linkedin by the people who are trying to fill the vacancies. It doesn't mean that this is a complete listing of jobs that are available. You will have to check other on-line sources for that.

With Linkedin, you can search for members that share similar titles as the job you are interested in applying for.

The advantage to doing so is that you can look at their profile to see if there are any ideas or content that you could leverage for your profile, that is to add to it.

IN THE GRAPHIC BELOW, I CLICKED ON THE ***PEOPLE LINK***, THEN ENTERED ***Health and Safety Specialist*** as my search term.

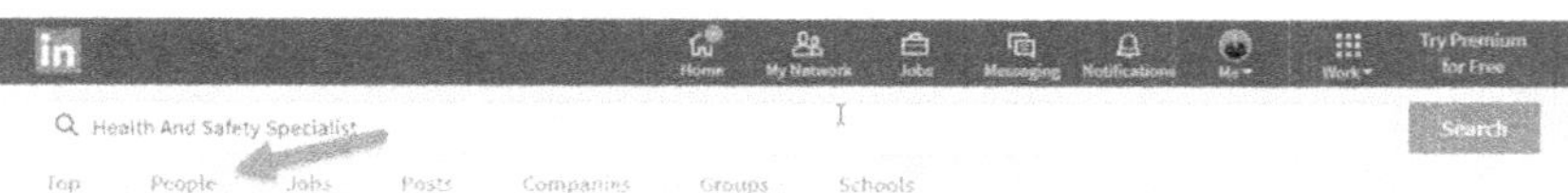

There is value in checking out the profiles of people that you have connected with on Linkedin. Perhaps they may have something posted that could be a resource to you by way of added knowledge or a connection to somebody that could forward your job-searching activities.

In addition, it is worthwhile doing a search for the company or organization that you are interested in or have applied for. You can gain some interesting insights about them if they have a company Linkedin profile set up. This could be the kind of information that would help you in a job interview with them, perhaps even insider information.

To conclude ... this chapter, how to leverage Linkedin for job-searching, is easily a subject that we could spend a lot of time on.

Like every other aspect of your job-searching strategies, that is developing your resumes, building a network and a team of references, it is only one piece and it has to be consistent with everything else. Make sure you take the time to develop your profile fully and start building and leveraging your connections.

Remember the concept of ***Givers Gain*** ... a concept developed by Dr. Ivan Misner, Founder of Business Networking International. If you ***give*** something or a service to someone else, ***without*** the expectation of something in return, the odds are that you will ***receive*** something in return.

This can be something as simple as sending an article to someone who you think might benefit from it or perhaps writing an informational article on a subject you are experienced in. And what you receive in return, doesn't necessarily come from someone who you have given to. It could be a connection of theirs or perhaps a complete stranger.

Some might call it Karma, others might call it the Law of Attraction in action. Either way, it is a good value and practice to develop.

In the next section, we create strategies to maximize your references.

SECTION II

JOB SEARCH — REFERENCE STRATEGIES

1. JOB-SEARCH – REFERENCE STRATEGIES

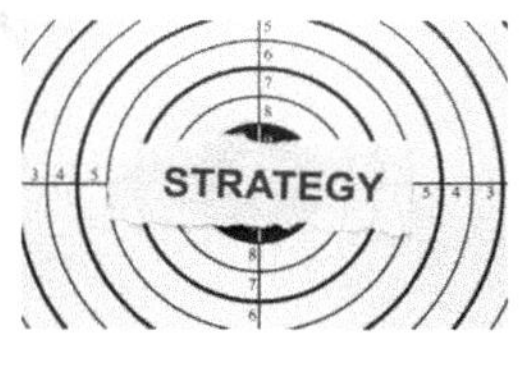

In this section, we look closely at how to strategize and use your references effectively.

The right list of personal references can be the key to success in securing follow up interviews.

Each reference should:

- Consent to give a reference about you.
- Have a surname different than yours (even if unrelated).
- Work in an office where he or she can receive calls during business hours and can privately ***tell*** (rhymes with "sell") about you intelligently, credibly, and enthusiastically.
- Be thoroughly prepared by you to give a *knowledgeable, motivational, inspirational* reference.

Additional Reference Attributes:

As you create your list of preference references, besides being a cheerleader for you as to how wonderful you are, look for these additional attributes:

- A successful professional life.
- A self confident, upbeat, outgoing demeanour.
- Good oral and written communication skills.
- A fondness for you (with a little PR, if necessary).
- A desire, (preferably burning) to help you succeed.

Remember, you have a wide field to draw from in order to pick perfect professional references.

By only considering former supervisors or college instructors as references, most job seekers neglect 80 percent of the potential reference population.

Who could be your influential references?

Review your career history and your current business contacts for the names of influential references who can give you ***search security*** without ***job jeopardy***. Your list might include:

- Former supervisors.
- Your boss's boss and other high-level executives at past employers who knew your contributions.
- Co-workers at present or past employers who witnessed your skills and effectiveness.
- Subordinates who can verify your management ability.

- Colleagues or others who served with you on committees or task forces.
- Members of trade associations or other professional groups who know you.

If you haven't already, generate a list of potential references that meet the above criteria.

In the next chapter, we look at matching your references to specific jobs that you are applying for.

2. MATCH YOUR REFERENCES TO THE TARGET JOB

Our next step is to take the names from the lists that you generated after reading the last chapter and match those references to your target job.

For each prospective position, pick a back-up team of *specialty* references.

These people have special knowledge of:

- The target company
- Influential people at the target company
- The industry in which the company is involved
- Influential people in the industry whose names can be used
- The particular skills required which you possess

Line Up the Defence

No matter how you plan to play your references, follow protocol. (It's not just polite. It's the only way to win.)

When you intend to give a reference's name to an interviewer, or at the very least, as soon as you have, *inform* the reference of that fact! Provide them information about:

- Who may be calling
- From what company
- About what position

IN THE NEXT CHAPTER, WE LOOK AT HOW YOU CAN PREPARE YOUR references for when they are called to talk about you.

3. PROFESSIONAL REFERENCE QUESTIONS LIST

Before you call upon your references to put them to work, you should help make it easier for them by providing them with a copy of **the Professional Reference Questions List** or the **Personal Reference Questions List as applicable.**

They're included in your Resource Section at the end of this book.

Let's look at the one for Professional references first.

The idea behind these lists is for you to make it easier for your references to *rave* about you.

You will notice that some of the questions are requesting some factual information from your references and others are asking for their opinion.

The idea would be to consult with your references before you go for an interview and help them fill out the form. Some might appreciate your help, others may not.

. . .

The Professional Reference Questions List

How long have you known?

Hopefully, the people you have chosen for references have known you for some time.

How do you know?

This question is asking your reference in what capacity do they know you.

Did they work along side of you in a particular job?

Did they supervise you?

Did you supervise them?

The *strength* of your reference is *increased* if they are able to demonstrate that they have a good idea of how you work.

When was he/she hired?

You would likely need to provide this information for your reference, especially if you are no longer working with them.

When did he/she leave?

The same applies to this question.

If you no longer work with this particular reference, provide them the date that you left employment with them.

What was his/her salary when he/she left?

Odds are that you will have to provide this as they wouldn't likely know.

Why did he/she leave?

You can provide your reference with the details as to why you left, assuming that you did leave of course. Your reference should rephrase your answer to this question into their own words. That is, something they would be comfortable saying.

Did you work with him/her directly?

This appears to be a fairly simple question.

The Hiring Manager is basically qualifying the reference as to how well they probably knew you. If your reference didn't actually work that closely with you, its not really a problem if the reference is able to describe what your working relationship was.

A Hiring Manager may give more credibility to a reference that has worked *closely* with you rather than one that you had a *passing* acquaintance with.

Was he/she usually on time?

Your reference may not know the answer to this one, so I would tell them to say something like "I'm not really sure about that."

"I can't say that I noticed anything related to that."

It's somewhat of an evasive answer but probably better then them saying "Oh yeah, he was late all the time!" You're not going to win any points with a response like that one.

Was he/she absent from work very often?

Your reference may not know the answer to this question.

If you haven't been absent from work a lot, you may want to impress upon your reference that you pride yourself on being able to make it to work regularly. Likely, the Hiring Manager will want to hear something like that.

If you have been absent from work quite a bit recently and over the not so distant past, you may want to come up with some kind of an explanation as to why you were sick. Your personal health is confidential and of nobody else's business, however a sick time record can work against you when it comes to getting hired.

Did his/her personal life ever interfere with his/her work?

Whoever is checking out your references shouldn't likely be able to ask this question, but don't be surprised if they do. The best answer would be "No, not that I am aware of."

What were his/her titles?

This is a simple question to identify what your job title was. Make sure that your reference is matched with the particular job title you had at the time.

The Hiring Manager is also likely checking up on you to see if the job title that you actually had, is the same as the one you have identified in your resume.

What were his/her duties?

You may have to explain them to your reference.

If they were had the same job duties as you, they would obviously know them. Others may not though.

The challenge here is that your reference may not have a clear understanding of what your duties were. If you provide them a list and they just read the list off, its not going to look very good for you.

Another consideration is that the Hiring Manager when contacting your references, may want to dig a little deeper about what you have written on your resume. If your reference has an in-depth knowledge of you and your job duties, then well great. If not, your reference might be better off coming up with an evasive answer.

Did he/she cooperate with supervisors?

This is a loaded question.

The desired answer would be "*of course*!"

Did he/she cooperate with co-workers?

This leads to similar answer as above. You will want to make it seem that you get along well with everyone.

Did he/she take work home very often?

Its hard to say how to answer this one.

On one hand, bringing work home can look like you are a *dedicated, diligent worker*, willing to go the extra step to get something done.

On the other hand, bringing work home could indicate that you have a problem with completing your work during your working hours. It could also indicate a worker that is having work vs home issues.

You could appear to be *out of balance* if you are doing *work at work* and *work at home*.

What are his/her primary attributes?

This leads to a subjective answer from your references. They will have to come up with their own answer.

Hopefully it will be a glowing, positive one about you.

What are his/her primary liabilities?

This is similar to the last one. They will have to come up with their own answer.

The problem is that this might work against you, so it might be wise to offer a rather small liability but illustrate how you are *currently* resolving it.

So, what you are doing is turning a ***weakness*** into a ***strength***. You'll have to share this with your reference of course.

Is he/she eligible for rehire? If your reference is a co-worker, they wouldn't likely be able to answer this. But if your reference is your manager they would likely know.

Let's hope they say yes. Otherwise, you should probably be looking for another reference.

Can you confirm the information he/she has given?

Your reference will have to wait and see what they are asked.

In the next chapter, we look at a ***Personal Reference Questions List***, for friends and colleagues.

4. PERSONAL REFERENCE QUESTIONS LIST

This list is one that you will use for references that are more of the *personal* nature.

These are friends or perhaps people that you have worked with in a voluntary capacity. They would have a good idea of what you are like, outside of work and would do a good job of referring you.

While it is helpful that these references know what job it is that you are applying for and what your background is that makes you believe that you can do the job, they *don't* need an *in depth* understanding of the job.

They just need to be able to talk about how it was working alongside of you. They also need to be able to speak concisely and clear. You don't want somebody as a referral who gets tongue-tied under pressure.

~

The Personal Reference Questions List

How long have you known?

Make sure your reference has an answer for this question.

A long-winded "well let me see. My son was three at the time and now he's eight. But wait a minute ... my daughter was two when we met. I remember him coming to her birthday party. No ... wait that can't be right!"

Their answer should be *short and sweet.*

How do you know?

You and your reference need to agree where it was you met.

Did you work together on a volunteer project or serve on a non-profit board of directors?

What is your opinion of?

This is a subjective answer on the part of your reference of course.

Hopefully, they think highly of you and do some cheerleading on your behalf as part of their response to the question.

Does he/she get along well with others?

As in the previous questions for your professional references, you want your answer to be "yes, you do!"

Is he/she usually on time?

Your personal reference may not know how to answer this one.

Is he/she absent from work very often?

The same as the previous question, they may not know anything about your working conditions.

Does he/she bring work home very often?

Probably best to answer "I don't really know."

Does he/she like his/her job?

If you are currently employed and looking for another job, it would be worthwhile for your personal reference to understand that 'of course you like your current job' but you are looking to improve yourself through a job change.

You wouldn't want them saying that you don't like your job or hate it, as that won't help your case at all.

What are his/her primary attributes?

They can prepare for this question on their own.

What are his/her primary liabilities?

Encourage your reference to come up with something mild.

This isn't the time to draw attention to your major short-comings. There is nothing wrong with having them, we all do. But the Hiring Manager doesn't need to know them at this point.

In the next chapter, we look at strategies to be proactive in your job searching and put your references to work, even before they are called by an employer checking up on you.

5. GO ON THE OFFENSE

You needn't wait for your employers to call before you put your references into the game.

Those specialized ***preference references*** can write or phone the prospect to give your prospects a boost.

Here's how.

Letters That Lock in the Target

A ***second***, post-interview letter ***must*** be:

A ***super-reference***, written by the ***right*** person, targeted to the ***right*** person (***a decision maker***), and containing marketable information about your abilities and skills.

What someone *says* about you has *ten times* the influence of what you say about yourself.

Use a ***brief***, perfectly drafted one-page letter --- from a *carefully* selected reference as a cover letter for your resume.

Personalize each letter to individuals inside the target company(ies) who either have:

- The *authority* to hire you, or
- *Connections* to those who do.

The key is positioning.

The ***position*** of your reference, the way you are ***positioned*** by your reference in a letter or telephone call, targeting a ***specific*** position, and someone in a ***position*** to hire for it, are all essential elements of a super-reference.

To position yourself for the perfect position, choose a reference who is the best position to write the best positioning letter for you.

Who Should Write?

Selection of the reference cover letter writer is the first element of positioning.

He or she should be:

- Someone who knows the recipient of the letter
- Someone who knows someone else the recipient knows
- Someone who, by reputation, is known to the recipient of the letter
- Someone whose letterhead, title, and responsibilities will attract the recipient's attention or give ***credibility*** to the statements in the letter --- and to you

Help Them Say the Right Thing

Most references simply haven't a clue when it comes to writing the perfect letter.

That's why typical reference letters are ridiculous. References aren't particularly good learners, either. After all, if they weren't more important than you, you wouldn't need them to lend you their importance, right?

It's not only their belief --- it's yours.

So rather than try to teach them or leave the letters' impact to chance, write your *perfect* letters *yourself*! The result is a far more detailed, consistent presentation, and your references will probably be relieved.

Just ask. You'll probably hear: "Sure, whatever you want. Just type it up and I'll sign it."

If the reference is a personal friend or colleague well known to the target, the opening and closing paragraphs should be in the writer's own words. But you can help by supplying the language for the *value* paragraph.

When you let your references know of the impending reference check, let them in on your excitement too. Fill your reference in on what you've learned from the interview and what kind of call he or she can expect, from what kind of person.

Don't coach your references so well that they sound "canned," but do be sure that each one understands:

- The objectives of your job search
- The specific knowledge that you'd like him or her to relate in a reference call
- The delivery necessary for maximum impact on the reference checker

Ask your references to accept the telephone calls or return them immediately (you'll pay any toll charges), and to notify you of the details the moment they hang up. You need the feedback and you need it fast.

Always re-contact your references after they've made their play in your behalf to:

- Express your gratitude and appreciation
- Ask about their impression of your prospective employer ---

and your prospects
- Express your gratitude and appreciation. Again.

IN THE NEXT SECTION, WE LOOK AT HOW TO HANDLE THE INITIAL PHONE call.

SECTION III

THE INITIAL PHONE CALL

1. THE INITIAL PHONE CALL

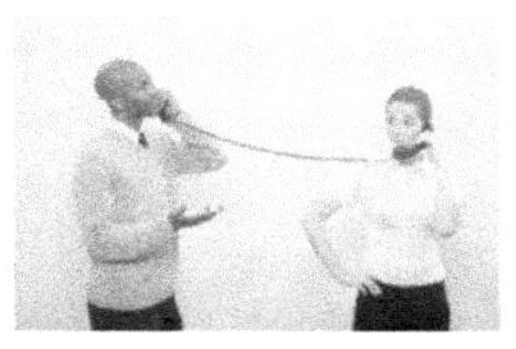

Your resume wowed them!! They want to speak with you in person. Now what?

The interview process starts from the *very first* phone call that the prospective employer makes to you to arrange for an interview.

Be prepared! You are being judged!

If you aren't available to take a phone call *live and in person*, your telephone answering machine, yes, some people still do have them or your voice mail, should have an *appropriate*, *professional* sounding greeting. When you are job searching, it isn't the time to have a catchy novelty telephone greeting.

Have pen & paper at the ready.

Have easy access to your personal agenda or commitments so that you can readily arrange for an interview appointment. Be prepared to ask them some quick questions in return.

Questions You Need to Ask:

Here are some questions to ask while you have them on the phone or in an e-mail if that was their initial contact method:

- time & location?
- who will be conducting the interview?
- what format will the interview be?
- are there other people being interviewed for the job? [you might want to be careful with this question though]
- is there anything that you need to bring with you?

IN OUR NEXT SECTION, WE LOOK AT *PREPARING* FOR YOUR FIRST interview.

SECTION IV

The First Interview

1. THE FIRST INTERVIEW

Welcome to Section IV, the first interview.

In an Employer's attempt to fill a staffing vacancy, they may interview *any number* of people and they may interview an individual *a number* of times before they make their mind up as to who they will hire.

This chapter addresses your first interview for a *specific* job application.

We look at some things you ***should*** do and some that you ***shouldn't***.

We look at what you should *expect* in this first interview and some suggestions on how to answer interview questions.

In *later* sections of the program, we dig even deeper into interviewing tactics and strategies.

While this section focuses on it being your *first* interview, you need to be aware that it might be the only one that the Employer plans on conducting. So, you need to do your best at every step of the interview process.

Here are some interview formats that you may encounter:

Individual Interviewer - You may find yourself being interviewed by only one person.

Team Interview (panel) - In a panel interview you may find yourself facing 3 or more interviewers. They will have prepared in advance a series of interview questions to ask you. As one asks you a question, the others will be scoring you on how you answer.

They will likely take turns asking you the questions. And they will have assigned a rating to each question. Upon completion of the interview they will compare scores and then *rate* you against others competing for the same job.

Team with other applicants - Team interviews can be quite challenging. You will likely be interviewed at the same time as a number of other potential candidates. You could find yourself sitting on chairs placed in a circle.

THE INTERVIEWERS WILL HAVE CREATED A NUMBER OF QUESTIONS IN advance. They likely have other criteria in mind as well as a way to determine your suitability for hire. They could be looking for how you get along with the others in the interview group.

They could be looking for *natural* leadership abilities to emerge from this group interview or even *how* you respond to pressure.

ON CAMERA - YOU COULD WALK INTO THE INTERVIEW ROOM TO FIND A camera facing you and perhaps a number of television/monitor screens with interviewers located at remote locations.

INTERVIEWS CONDUCTED ON SKYPE OR BY CONFERENCE CALLS ARE becoming more mainstream these days.

. . .

Dress for Success

Will Rogers said, "I never met a man I didn't like."

An employment interview is a place to be liked. Unless you're likeable, you won't be hireable.

When job hunting, dress for success.

In job-hunting, first impressions are critical.

Remember, you are marketing a product -- *yourself* -- to a potential employer. And the first thing the employer sees when greeting you is your attire.

Therefore, you must make every effort to have the proper dress for the type of job you are seeking.

The old saying 'never judge a book by its cover' may be a good one, but interviewers are human like everybody else and likely to act upon their *first* impressions. So, you want to make sure that you are giving a good one.

In the next chapter, we look at how to organize your presentation or responses in your upcoming interview.

2. ORGANIZING YOUR PRESENTATION

This chapter is on **Organizing Your Presentation** and offers tips on how to answer job interview questions.

You might be wondering why I'm using the term *'presentation'* at all.

I think it is helpful to think of each of your interview questions as being mini speeches or presentations.

It might seem a little out of order with this lesson, but the idea is that you give it some thought and practice before the interview process is upon you.

Here are some sure-fire formulas of organizing your responses to the interviewer's questions.

Past, Present, Future

Here is an example ... "in the ***past*** I would have handled the situation this way...

Recently I experienced a similar situation and this is how I handled it.

I learned from it and here is ***how*** I would handle it should I encounter it again."

Here's another possible outline:

Problem/Cause/Solution

- The problem is...
- The problem is caused by ...
- Some solutions are ...
- The best solution is ...

Let's look at an example of using the **Problem/Cause/ Solution** outline:

"From my ***perspective***, the problem seems to be blah, blah, blah.

I ***believe*** that it is caused by blah, blah, blah.

From my ***experience***, there are several different solutions to this problem. We could blah, blah, blah or another way might be to blah, blah, blah.

I believe the ***best*** solution is to blah, blah, blah.

That last one is a different blah, blah, blah from the previous ones of course. 😁

The idea with using this outline is that you want to showcase yourself as an *expert* and that you are *capable* of *independent, strategic* thinking.

Dale Carnegie's Magic Formula

Before we look at his formula, some of you might be wondering who he is.

He wrote a book titled ***How to Win Friends and Influence People*** that was first published in 1936, it has sold over ***30 million copies world-wide*** and went on to be named #19 on *Time Magazine*'s list of ***100 most*** influential books in 2011.

His formula is **Example, Point, Reason.**

Let's look at how the formula would work.

Example: Give details of an incident that graphically illustrates your main idea.

Example: "This company has had some challenges with the people they are hiring. They keep leaving."

Point: Tell exactly what you want your audience to do.

Example: "You should hire me now and pay me a good salary so that I will stay longer than the others."

Reason: Highlight the advantage or benefit to be gained when they do what you ask them to do.

Example: "I am a proven dedicated and loyal employee, with a long history of quality service and you would be stupid if you didn't hire me."

Okay, that example is tongue and cheek. While it is something you might love to do in an interview, I wouldn't suggest it.

However, it does illustrate example, point, reason.

Every presentation regardless of its length, should have these three components:

- Opening
- Body
- Closing

Your opening and your closing should take about 15% of your time, so a total of 30%.

The remaining of your time, 70% is the body, where you expand upon your content.

If you were delivering a speech, the opening is where you would grab your audience's attention. I call it 'wake em, up... shake em up!"

You can't quite do that when answering an interview question.

Your interviewer would probably think you are crazy if you started yelling at them. But what you can do in your opening when answering an interview question is to set the stage for the fact that you actually know something about this question and you are prepared to speak about it.

As for the ***body*** of your answer, this is where you provide the *details* of your answer.

An effective ***conclusion*** to an interview question can be to do a *quick summary* of your response and something to the effect that your response is over and you are ready for the next question.

We will go into greater detail about how to answer interview questions in Section VI.

But before we do, the next chapter provides an overview of the interviewing process.

3. YOU GOT AN INTERVIEW. NOW WHAT?

Let's look at the job interview process, starting off with your first interview.

In my part of the world where we have a tight job market, just getting to the interview stage can be like winning a lottery.

Your resume likely got you to the interview stage. So, what happens now?

The goal for this first face to face encounter is to win a second one.

Tell yourself *beforehand* that you need to come away with a good sense of the most effective techniques and timing for this target.

Then when you are inside the prospective employer's office:

Be Observant

Throughout the interview, *look and listen* to gather information that will help you.

A successful interview requires the ability to think on your feet, metaphorically speaking of course. You will more than likely be sitting down for your interview.

Your undivided attention is necessary to seize opportunities as they arise.

Take Out Your Well-Organized Notebook and Jot Down Notes

It makes you look professional. Write names, titles, buzzwords, products, and other items you can use in the follow up stage.

Don't reduce your eye contact with the interviewer; don't ask him or her to repeat anything or how to spell something.

You *can* and *should* ask questions. Not only do the right questions help you control the interview, but by asking them, you elicit information to fuel your follow up.

Ask the right questions. Don't ask personal controversial or negative questions of any kind. Stay away from asking anything that will lead into sensitive areas.

Invariably, salary and benefits should be avoided.

Nowadays, you can often gather quite a bit of information about the organization you are applying to by doing a search on the internet. It will be expected that you have *some* understanding of their business.

While some knowledge will certainly be helpful, a *lack* of knowledge or asking questions that you should already know the answers to, could work against you.

Here are examples of benign questions that may have a favourable impact:

- How many employees does the company have?
- What are the company's plans for expansion?
- Is the business operated as a proprietorship or a non-profit?
- What is the supervisor's management style?
- What is the supervisor's title?

- Who does the supervisor report to?
- Are you ready and able to hire now?
- How long will it take to make a hiring decision?
- How long has the position been open?
- How many employees have held the position in the past five years?
- Why are the former employees no longer in the position?
- What does the company consider the five most important duties of the position to be?
- What do you expect the employee you hire to accomplish?

Jot some key words and concepts from these questions and answers into a page of a small notebook.

We go into greater detail on questions that you could/should ask your interviewer in Section VII.

In our next chapter, we will prepare to use some tactics that will turn the interview in your favour.

4. JOB INTERVIEW DOS

In this chapter, we look at a job interview check list that aims at helping you with turning the job interview to your *advantage.*

Job Interview Check-list

Interview "Dos"

Schedule for success: Quite often you are provided with a time for your interview. The interviewers have scheduled it for their convenience, that is to fit into their schedule.

If it works for you ... *good,* go for it. Just make sure you leave enough time for you to travel to the interview allowing time for any problems or obstacles that arise.

Avoid meal interviews: Meal interviews tend to be awkward affairs. You need to be on your best behaviour if you must have one. You are likely being *judged* on your social behaviour as much as your job skills.

It is also difficult to answer questions at the same time as you are trying to eat your meal. A busy restaurant can make it very difficult to participate in an interview.

Having said all that ... there are some business owners that want to 'break bread' with a potential job applicant, so they can see what they are like in an informal setting.

Arrive alone and on time. Don't arrive early. Acclimate to your environment. A job interview isn't the time to bring your mother, father or significant other.

You are the one being interviewed, not them!

Plan to arrive at the interview meeting's location no more than 5 to 10 minutes before your meeting is scheduled. It could be awkward for you if the interviewers have scheduled their interviews to close together and you find yourself sitting beside another applicant.

Acclimating to your environment means getting comfortable before you get called in for the interview. If you are wearing a coat and/or a hat, remove them. Be ready to start your interview as soon as you are invited in.

Remember the concept of ***first impressions***.

Carry an attaché case. The time of the attaché case has likely come and gone, unless you are a secret agent or a financial courier where you will likely be handcuffed to one.

Nowadays, there are inexpensive, small soft-shelled file/notebook computer bags that work quite well for carrying a notebook, pens and whatever else you might need for your interview.

Eliminate fear of the unknown. This takes some work on your part. You should research the company you are applying for work at so that you won't be caught off guard with a question about their company.

The old saying of 'knowledge is power' comes into play here. The more you know about the company ***the better***.

Talking to current or former employees can be helpful to learn what type of interview questions might be asked.

Make the first impression the best. This is the time to muster up your courage and project a sense of power, self-control and self-confidence. As we have said before, dress for success.

Make this first impression a *memorable* one, in the right way of course!

Greet the interviewer properly. When meeting somebody for the first time, the *expectation* is to shake their hand. If the interviewer doesn't offer their hand first, *go for it*! Offer yours!

It might help that *positive* first impression that you are aiming at.

Depending on the time of day a greeting such as 'Good morning ...' Good afternoon' followed by something to the effect of 'I'm pleased to meet you' is acceptable.

Hone your handshake. We talked about handshakes in a previous chapter. Hopefully you have been practicing and are comfortable with shaking someone's hand.

Avoid assuming a subordinate role. By some people's estimation, you *are* in a subordinate role.

They have the *job*, you *want* the job. They have the *power*, you *don't* have the power. That likely works for them, it's their rules. It's time to change the rules, in your favour. You wouldn't have been invited in for the interview if they hadn't thought you were a *worthy* applicant.

That *gives* you power. They have a *problem* to solve. They need to hire somebody that will make them look good. You are a possible *solution*. More *power* for you.

While you are being interviewed and asked questions, if you are able to, use a part of your mind to take a look at what is happening in the interview. Monitor yourself.

Ask yourself if you are being passive or actively engaged in the questions?

In the next section, we look at Interviewer personalities. Some will *want* you to be subordinate to them, others *won't* appreciate it.

Have your script well-rehearsed. When you think of script you might be thinking about an actor's lines for a play that they are in. In this case, your script would be your answers that you have practiced in advance for questions that you expect to answer.

Attempt to sit next to or near the Interviewer. Given a choice of seating, it is probably better to sit nearer to your Interviewer rather than further.

Hopefully, the Interviewer isn't sitting behind a big desk, serving as a tool to make them feel important. Some interviews are held at a table. Sitting across from your Interviewer would be better than sitting beside them.

Take notes.

The idea here is to take some notes to jog your memory after the interview. The challenge of course is to have your note recording, not take away from your being asked questions and you answering them.

It could work against you if the Interviewer believes you are easily distractible.

Have an extra copy of your resume with you in case the Interviewer doesn't have it.

It can also come in handy if you need to refer to it to answer an interview question.

Educational background questions: Show what you know! Each of us has different educational backgrounds. Make use of yours in answering your interview questions. *Show* them that you *know you know*.

Character questions: Be careful! We discuss these at length in an upcoming section.

You will want to answer these types of questions carefully so that you look good.

Initiative and creativity questions: Focus on what and why. I'm reminded of an interview question used by an HR colleague of mine that used to work in the aeronautical field. "How many ping pong balls does it take to fill a 747?

How could anybody possibly know that answer. But a close one would be 'I suppose it would depend if you took the seats out or not.'

The business that she worked for was refitting used 747 airliners and turning them into mail delivery planes. So, the comment about taking the seats out to fit in more, was a valid one.

In this case the HR Manager was looking for *creative thinking* and to see if a *thought-provoking* challenge caused any problems for the applicant.

This would be an example of a thinking *out of the box* answer that we hear about so often.

There was no right or wrong answer.

Career and objective questions: Make it clear what they hear. Since the *career and objective statements* have been dropped from usage on our resumes, in favour of *positioning statements*, we need to make it clear to our interviewers, what our plans are.

In an upcoming chapter, we will discuss ***career*** and ***objective*** questions. You might hear them in the form of "where do you see yourself in five years?"

Admire something in the Interviewer's office. You can use this technique to bond with your interviewer. You have to be genuine in doing so though.

If you see something that resonates with you, go for it. If you don't, don't force it. You will come across as phony and it will take away from your interview.

Assess the Interviewer's style. In the next section, we look at four different styles of Interviewer's personalities. They aren't the only four and what we talk about may not always hold true, but it does help you in advance to be prepared for whatever you encounter.

"Mirror" the Interviewer's body language, facial expressions, eye movement, rate of speech, tone of voice and rate of breathing. This is a good technique to master, whether you use it in your interview or interactions with other people. It will only work when dealing with an individual, not a group.

The idea behind the technique is that if you use the same or similar style of communication as the other person does, they in turn will feel that you are resonating with them. As the saying goes, they feel you are on the same wave length.

As mental health therapist, I have good response using the technique when interacting with people that would likely otherwise be hostile to me. The challenge is that you don't want to come across as being patronizing or condescending, as that will work against you.

Align with the Interviewer. A job interview *isn't* the place to get into a philosophical argument with your Interviewer. *Agreeing* with their perspective, assuming that you do, can help position you in their mind higher than someone who disagrees with them or is argumentative.

Use "insider" language. If you are applying for a position that you have previously worked in, you likely have gathered a lot of insider language that you can use in your answers. If you haven't worked in the specific field that you are applying for, you can likely help yourself by doing on-line research on the industry.

Using *insider language* helps position you as an *experienced* applicant or at least *knowledgeable* about the field you are applying. You want to be able to score every point that you possibly can in your interview. Insider language can help to do so.

Find an area of agreement and lead slowly and carefully to the offer. When you are being asked questions by the interviewer, this may be difficult to do as you are on the defence.

When it comes to *your* turn to ask questions it might be a little easier. The areas of agreement would hopefully be that you would be the *suitable candidate* for the job vacancy. If you are able to pull it off, they may offer you the job on the spot, pending their following up with checking your references.

Be honest, not modest. If you done it, it ain't bragging. Give yourself credit for what you have done and use that experience for *leverage* to solve the employer's problem.

Say positive things about your present (former) employer. You can almost guarantee that your Interviewer will be on high alert for anything that you say about your former or current employer. The belief is that if you are eager to bad-mouth them, you would likely do so with your new employer and that certainly wouldn't make you a good hire.

Admire the achievements of the prospective employer. This is where your pre-interview research can come in handy. If you come up with a gem, fit it in at the appropriate time. Just be sure that you come across as being genuine.

Be observant. In any discussion, there can be multiple levels taking place. You might not know what is going on behind the scene, but perhaps the Interviewer might drop hints that you should be attuned to. It's kind of like using insider knowledge to your advantage.

Review your notes. This would be after the interview of course.

Limit interview to two hours. Hmmm, while it is suggested here, I'm not so sure how much control you have over the timing. Perhaps a more complex or demanding job may require a longer interview meeting but it is often divided up into several meetings with different people doing the interviewing.

At the end of the interview thank them for their time, shake hands again, and tell them you hope to hear from them soon. Politeness and manners go a long way in life. Ending the interview and leaving on a *positive note* may make the difference in hiring you or not, it they are undecided.

As we said earlier about not getting a *second* chance about a *first* impression, in this case we are getting a second chance to make an impression. Make it count!

These are all factors to take into consideration to help you become the *successful* job applicant.

Of course, you still need to wow them with your interview question answers.

In the next chapter, we explore some things that you really ***don't want to do*** during your job interview.

5. INTERVIEW DON'TS

We just looked at some strategies that we *should* do in preparation and during the interview. Now let's look at some interview **Don'ts.**

Interview "Don'ts"

Don't wear a coat, hat, or other outdoor clothing into the interview. There is usually an outer office area that you can remove your outdoor clothing *prior* to going into the interview room.

Taking off your outdoor clothing, once invited into the interview room would likely be awkward but it also takes away those vital first few minutes you have to make a good first impression.

Don't wait more than half an hour for the Interviewer. While this might be proactive advice, I would say that it depends on the situation. If I were told that the Interviewer is delayed by unavoidable circumstances, but *really wants* to interview me, I would likely stay.

If I was under the impression that it *didn't seem* that there was much priority in the interviewer showing up in time, I might hit the road. I would advise the receptionist or administrative assistant to reschedule the interview if I did decide to leave.

The reality of this situation is that it depends on how much personal power you have. If you truly believe that you are in a power situation, it may be worth your while to leave.

If you aren't in a position of power and really, really need the job, you might want to be a little more tolerant and stick around for a while.

Don't address the Interviewer by his or her first name. At least, not at first.

If they offer and invite you to call them by their first name, feel free to do so.

Otherwise, stick with a formal address Mr. or Ms. ___ whatever their surname is.

Don't use trite phrases and/or tired clichés. Many phrases tend to be tied into the area of the country you live in.

A tired cliché is a saying that may have had some meaning in the past, but has lost its meaning and has become meaningless words.

Some that come to mind are:

... and Bob's your uncle.

... you know what I mean...

... and so on and so forth...

I'm sure that you can think of some that you have heard many times. The word **Like** has taken on a life of its own for at least one generation.

Don't smoke. I'm sure that in the so-called olden days, the Interviewer might even offer you a smoke, but those days are long gone.

If you do smoke, try not to smoke before coming in for the interview.

A non-smoker can easily smell if you have and you may have blown the interview even before you have started.

Don't chew gum. Short version ... it is considered to be unprofessional.

Don't interrupt. There is an old joke that goes ...**The Boss's Rules:** Rule One, the Boss is always right. Rule Two ... see Rule One.

It's the Interviewer's show. Like the boss, you need to *let* them think they are right. That doesn't mean that you can't correct them if they are wrong, just don't cut them off when they are speaking. They will likely consider you to be rude and that will work against you.

Don't object to discriminatory questions.

In an upcoming section, we look at questions that may be discriminatory in nature.

There may be proactive ways to answer the question without strongly objecting. Just because there may be laws to prevent discriminatory questions, doesn't mean that it won't happen.

If you are of a particular group that may face discrimination and you actually do encounter it in a job interview, you may want to give some thought as to whether you really want to work for this organization.

You have to wonder, if they are discriminatory in a job interview, what would the working conditions be like on a regular basis? You may change your mind about wanting to work for them.

Don't look at your watch. I haven't worn a watch in years since smart phones came out. I can't recall that I have seen anybody else wearing a watch lately.

If you happen to be a person that does wear a watch, looking at it during your interview can work against you. It looks like you have a time commitment to be somewhere else and are not present in the moment.

Don't read any documents on the Interviewer's desk. This would seem to be one of those common-sense type suggestions, but as the saying goes "common sense isn't so common."

Unless invited to read documents on the Interviewer's desk ... don't!

It looks like there are a lot less things you ***shouldn't*** be doing than what you ***should*** be doing.

~

IN THE NEXT SECTION, SECTION V, WE LOOK AT **FOUR BASIC Interviewer Personality Types** and offer strategies to levelling the playing field.

SECTION V

Four Basic Interviewer Personality Types

1. FOUR BASIC INTERVIEWER PERSONALITY TYPES: TYPE ONE

In this section, we look at how to recognize Four Basic Personality Types that you might encounter in a job interview.

There are likely several different models out there, but this one seems to work well.

Type 1 are Outgoing and Direct:

These people are called "socializers." They are energetic, friendly, and self assured.

To spot this personality, look for the following characteristics:

1. A flamboyant style of dress. Even in a conservative business suit, a brightly coloured tie, scarf, or jewelry might be worn. Current fashion is preferred to classic styles.

2. They likely have many pictures and personal mementos in the office.

3. They will have a cluttered desk, or at least a covered one.

4. They aren't very time conscious, so you might be kept waiting. In most cases, the Interviewer is juggling a hundred things at once.

These types gravitate toward personnel jobs because they're outgoing "people" people.

If you're a methodical, reserved type, you can get into trouble with Interviewers of this type. You'll have to smile, talk faster, and get to the point.

They have to like you before they'll listen to you. And listening isn't on their list.

If you're this type, be careful. You don't want to out talk, out smile or out interview the Interviewer!

IN THE NEXT CHAPTER, WE LOOK AT THE SECOND INTERVIEWER personality type.

2. TYPE 2: SELF CONTAINED & DIRECT

This type is referred to as the "director." "Dictator" is more descriptive, though.

These people differ from socializers because they're far more reserved and conservative.

Before unconventional computer kids started running companies, it was believed you had to be like this to make top management. They're still among the high achievers in every field.

Clues to this personality are:

1. They have a conservative, high quality, custom tailored wardrobe, impeccably worn.

2. They have a neat, organized work space. A few expensive personal desk accessories.

Perhaps one or two classic picture frames containing family photos. Nothing flashy. Everything is understated.

3. They have a firm handshake, but not much of a smile. Not as talk-

ative as the first type. They'll size you up critically and wait for you to make your mistakes.

4. Time conscious and annoyed when others are not. They are goal and bottom line oriented. They believe that all work and no play is the way to spend the day.

To get along with this type, be all business. Don't waste the Interviewer's time. Eliminate unnecessary words, and be sincere.

This type itches around "touchy feely" people. You won't find them saying, "Oh I just adore this." You shouldn't either.

Don't be intimidated, either. If you are, Director types will sense it and reject you immediately. Don't be defensive about weaknesses in your background. Just explain them by turning them into strengths.

In the next chapter, we look at the third Interviewer personality type.

3. TYPE 3: SELF CONTAINED & INDIRECT

Such people are called "thinkers" and might be found in analytical professions. They don't speak up, socialize, or editorialize. They go about their work quietly, and they get it done properly.

Evidence of this personality includes:

1. Uninteresting, understated clothes. Grey and beige predominate. Style and looks aren't a priority, function is. The person is nothing if not practical.

2. They have few personal items and "warm fuzzies."

3. This Interviewer's hand will probably dangle at the end of their wrist. Shake it any way. It will confirm your suspicions that he or she is a "thinker."

4. They are time conscious and work oriented. Their work ethic is just a strong as the Directors', but Thinkers don't want to run things, they are loners.

5. They will likely have an organized desk, with neatly arranged work. Maybe even a "to do" list with half the items crossed off.

This type of person is hard to draw out and may become annoyed if you try. If you're pushy and aggressive, the thinker gets withdrawn and your offer will be withheld.

Answer questions directly and succinctly. Volunteer as much information as the Interviewer needs to make a decision. Thinkers thrive on data, but they need time to analyze it, so don't rush.

In the next chapter, we look at the fourth Interviewer personality type.

4. TYPE 4: OUTGOING & INDIRECT

The most common word for this personality type is "helper." They're friendly, like socializers, but without the aggressiveness.

Helpers tend to gravitate toward "human resources"; they're the closest the business world gets to providing psychiatric social work for employees. Helpers take time to know you before the actual interview begins.

They're nice, but will do almost anything to avoid making a decision. In that area, you need to help them.

You're probably talking to a helper when there is:

1. A nonthreatening appearance that matches their demeanour. They wear natural shades and soft fabrics.

2. They have a number of personal items on the desk, often hand made. Their office will reflect that other people are important to them.

3. They have a friendly, expressive, and concerned approach. Helpers may apologize for keeping you waiting because they were busy solving everyone else's problems.

They smile warmly, reach out to take your hand, and might never let it go.

4. They will likely have a phone ringing, work piling up, and many uncompleted projects. To a helper, "people" are all that matters.

These people are the opposite of the "director"" type, and they rarely play opposite each other.

The helper never gives up trying to convince the director to "humanize," "personalize," and "realize".

To get hired, take time to establish rapport, become friends, and accentuate the importance of the "person" in "personnel." But remember to limit interviews to two hours.

With helpers, it's your responsibility to get your job qualifications across. If you don't, you may leave the interview with a friend but not a job.

They won't ask you to give them a reason to hire you or even recommend you for a second interview. Emotionally, they don't realize that's why you're there. They think its because you're taking a hiring survey. A helper helps ... but doesn't hire.

This is a remarkably accurate way to out stereotype the stereotypers. Some will fit the description exactly, others will fit several.

No matter. Just know and play to your audience. Study the four profiles and practice typecasting a few of your friends, coworkers, and relatives.

Learn to pick up on the clues to someone's predominant personality style. Then practice playing to them. They're your audience too.

Picking up clues from a person's appearance, speech, and body language can serve you in many ways throughout your career. In short, while you are concentrating on making a good impression, you also need to be absorbing a clear impression of everybody and everything else.

IN THE NEXT SECTION, SECTION VI, WE WILL DISCUSS COMMON interview questions and strategies on how to answer them.

SECTION VI

Common Interview Questions

1. COMMON INTERVIEW QUESTIONS

If you are applying for a job, any job, you can expect that you will be asked to participate in an interview. It could be face-to-face or could be over the phone, internet or Skype.

There are likely countless questions that you could be asked and some that you *shouldn't* be asked due to equal rights legislation etc.

Many employers have developed their own questions related to their specific field of business.

By practicing your responses to some of these questions, hopefully you will not be taken off guard if asked one of them.

Yes, there are lots of them provided here.

One of the best ways to deal with these questions, is to give some thought to how you would answer each of them. You will note that the questions have been organized into categories to help you focus and some of them seem to the same question, asked in different ways. They are!

You need to be able to think about each question that your Interviewer asks you.

What are they ***really*** asking you?

You may want to review Section IV: Chapter Two, where we explored several different methods of answering questions in general, but specifically interview questions.

If you are momentarily stumped by a question, don't panic. Ask the Interviewer if you could come back to that question later.

If the question truly does stump you, hopefully you will be able to think of a response while you are answering other questions.

I once went for a job interview and was peppered with 42 separate questions for over an hour and a half. My wife wasn't too thrilled as it was mid February in Canada, and she was sitting in the car waiting for me, freezing.

When you are practicing your responses, you should have somebody help you by asking you questions randomly from the list.

There can be a significant difference in how you answer a question ***in your mind*** and how you say it orally. Practice saying your answers out loud.

It can be helpful to record yourself on a recording device such as a smart phone for the audio or a camera that records video. You can then play back the question and response to determine if you might have handled it differently.

Most importantly, relax, go with the flow, and before you know it, you'll be in your next job.

I have broken the content of this section into categories of questions to try to keep it manageable.

Each category of questions will have its own chapter for simplicity.

Note: * Indicates that some background information or industry advice has been provided for you to consider.

2. INTERVIEW QUESTIONS TO ASSESS YOUR EDUCATION

- **How does your experience and education qualify you for this job?**

Select four to five accomplishments or skills based on what you have learned from the job description and the information you provided on your resumé.

- **How does your education qualify you for this job?**

This is basically the same question as the last one except focusing on your ***education***, excluding your experience. As the question asks, you should stay focused on your education that is *relevant* to the position you are applying for.

- **Why did you choose to attend the college that you are attending?** * This assumes of course that you are still in school. Be prepared for a follow-up question about your availability if you are still in school.

- **What aspect of your education applies to this position?**

This is another version of how does your education qualify you for this job.

- **What training have you received that qualifies you for this job?**

Training is a little different than your ***education***. It usually involves a shorter course period and the 'training' content tends to be hands on.

You can include any *live* training, that is you were *physically* present in the room with the trainer, or any on-line training you have taken such as with this course.

The idea remains that you need to be focused on the particular job that you are applying for.

- **What have you done outside of formal education to improve yourself?**

This would be a place to mention your training courses you have taken as in the previous question.

- **What training opportunities have you taken advantage of and why?**

This question adds a bit of a twist to the training question. It's asking for the courses but it is also asking you to *justify* why you took the courses.

Once again, you need to be focused on what training courses you mention as well as being able to provide your justification for taking them. 'It felt like a good idea at the time' probably wouldn't be a good answer.

- **What additional training will we have to provide for you if we hire you?**

This might be kind of a trick question. If you provide a list of areas that you need training in, you might come across as needing too much investment in you to hire you.

If you don't provide any suggestions, they may interpret it as you *not* having a clear understanding of the job they are offering.

One solution may be to say something to the effect that you will require a new-hire orientation to the job.

In the next chapter, we look at work experience questions.

3. WORK EXPERIENCE QUESTIONS

In this chapter, we look at **Work Experience Questions.** Starting off with ...

1. **Tell us about yourself.**

* [Focus on the aspects of your ***work experience*** that apply specifically to the position that you're applying for.

This can also take the form of, "if I asked one of your faculty members/previous supervisors to tell me about you, what would they say?"

Your answer should spotlight the education, experience, and work ethic that matches what the employer is seeking in an employee. End by saying you are *well prepared* for the position the interviewer is trying to fill.]

2. **What would you like me to know about you?**

* [Keep the answer ***short*** and ***power-packed.*** Identify four to five qualities that make you a strong candidate.

Highlight your academic achievements, ability to do the type of work you are interviewing for, and your work ethic.]

3. How are you qualified for this job?

I can't locate the source of this fact but I had read that if you have 75% of the qualifications required for any position, you will likely be eligible, at least for an interview.

This is your time to shine! Your response should be consistent with the info that you have featured in your resume.

4. How does your current job qualify you for this position?

If you are applying for an *internal* job, meaning that you already work for the company, this may be easy to answer. The Interviewer may have knowledge of your current job's duties.

If you work elsewhere, you will need to provide solid examples of how it will qualify you. Be prepared for a follow-up question of why are you wanting to leave your current position.

5. How does your experience qualify you for this job?

* [What have you done that prepares you for the responsibilities of this job?

Review what the employer is looking for (job description and any information a recruiter or career service staff member may have given you) and develop examples of how your academic work directly relates to the job responsibilities.]

6. Describe a typical day at your present position.

You may want to review your job description for your current position in preparation for this question being asked.

If your current job bores you, you may want to ignore that fact and show yourself in an optimistic, enthusiastic manner. Don't make yourself the hero of your story.

7. What were your three greatest accomplishments on your last job?

While you likely have personal accomplishments to mention, you would be better off giving examples of accomplishments that benefitted the employer.

You can take credit for the work that you did and you should, but it likely puts you in a better light if you show that you are willing to go the extra step to achieve an accomplishment that benefits the employer.

8. What are some of the things in your current job you have done well?

These should be featured in your resume, allowing you to pull them from there.

9. What is the most difficult assignment you have had?

This is a question that allows you to highlight your skills, however the Interviewer is likely looking at how you handled success or failure.

What did you learn from the assignment? What would you do differently?

10. What accomplishment on the job are you the most proud of?

Once again, you should probably use an example that benefitted the Employer in some way. You want to be seen as a team player, not a soloist.

11. What steps have you taken to improve your job skills?

You could focus on your continuing educational training as evidenced in the educational segment of your resume, assuming that you have of course.

12. What significant contributions have you made to the operation of your work group?

This question sets you up to show yourself as a team player.

13. How has your current position prepared you to take on greater responsibilities?

Maybe your current job has, or maybe it hasn't. As you go forward to interviewing for a new job, give some consideration to your current job.

What have been its advantages? What skills did you develop while in this job?

This should lead you to developing an answer relating to increased responsibility.

14. What makes you more qualified than the other candidates?

This isn't the time to be flippant and respond with "I'm smarter ... better looking ... desperate etc."

This is a difficult question to answer as you have no way of knowing the qualifications of the other candidates. The only real response you have available to you is to reinforce the qualifications and experience that you have to bring to the job.

15. Why do you want to leave your current job?

This is a question to be cautious of. You need to keep your response positive in nature.

If your reason for leaving is due to interpersonal conflict with co-workers or supervisors, you need to avoid commenting on it. If you do, the Interviewer may jump to the conclusion that you will likely do the same for them.

That doesn't make you a desirable hire.

The following two questions are versions of ones we looked at earlier.

16. How has your job prepared you to take on greater responsibility?

17. Tell us about your qualifications for this position.

The next two questions focus on your experience again:

18. What actions have you taken in the past 10 years to prepare you for this position?

19. What steps have you taken in the past two years to improve your qualifications?

However, this time they are looking for what *actions or steps* you have taken.

Once again, you can refer to the ***Experience*** section of your resume and come up with a comment that you are comfortable with saying to the effect that you believe in continually challenging yourself and building your skills.

20. In the areas where your experience falls short for this job, what steps will you take to make up for this shortfall?

This question is similar to an earlier one that asked what training are we going to have to provide you if we hire you?

The *difference* with this question is that they are looking for *you* to *analyze* your skill sets to see if you have shortcomings and how *you*, not them, are going to solve it.

21. Describe yourself.

This would be a good place to deliver an expanded version of your Summary Statement.

There is a value in developing your elevator pitch that includes your USP (Universal Sales Pitch) so that you could deliver it to respond to this question.

22. What skills and abilities do you have?

Once again, refer to the content of your resume.

You want to reinforce the fact that you have the skills to take on the job and you want to come across from a position of strength.

23. Recall an incident where you made a major mistake. What did you do after the mistake was made? What did you learn from this mistake?

This can be challenging to answer in that it starts off with having you look bad. Be careful what situation that you use to answer this one.

You need one that has a *teachable moment* as its outcome. "Well I certainly won't do that again!" isn't a good response.

The Interviewer is looking to see that you are capable of learning from your mistakes.

24. What is the greatest failure you've had? What would you have done differently?

This is another version of the previous question.

25. What action on the job are you the least proud of?

Give some serious thought as to how you will answer this one. It can backfire on you and shed negative light on you.

You don't want the Interviewer to think that is what your character is like, based on the one example you have given.

One way to answer it may be to provide a response that is fairly benign and then show how you *learned or grew* from the incident.

26. Tell us about a difficult situation that you encountered and how you resolved it.

This question is similar to others but is asking *how* you resolved it.

Your problem-solving skills are being assessed in this question. The Interviewer is looking to see if you used any kind of a problem-solving process and/or took a leadership position in solving the problem.

27. Where do you see yourself in five years?

* [The employer is asking the question because he or she wants to

know if you plan to go to work for one of their competitors after you complete your initial training.

Respond by letting the Interviewer know if you plan to stay in the position for which you are interviewing or to move up in the organization.]

In the next chapter we look at questions related to your resume.

4. RESUME RELATED INTERVIEW QUESTIONS

This chapter looks at resume-related questions.

- **Take us through your resume.**

This is an example of why you should have an extra copy of your resume with you when you go for the interview.

Starting off with your Summary Statement, you could read it word for word. Or you could give an expanded elevator pitch style of response.

Then you work your way through your experience that should reflect upon the job description and duties for the job you are applying for. Continue on with outlining your education that qualifies you for the job.

- **What are you most proud of on your resume?**

This is a question that you will have to answer on your own. Pride can get you in trouble and highlight you in a way that you don't want.

You would likely be better in choosing something that shares your pride with others, as in your part of being a team member on a specific project or perhaps sharing an accomplishment with others.

In the next chapter, we look at some general interview questions.

5. GENERAL INTERVIEW QUESTIONS

This chapter looks at interview questions that I have given the classification of General, as they don't seem to fit elsewhere.

Tell me a story.

* [Gear your stories to give the listener a feeling that you could fit in... you could do the job here.]

In what way do you think you can contribute to our company?

* [Preparing to answer this question requires a 2-step preparation: *assessing* your skills and *researching* the needs of the company.

An integral part of skill assessment (looking at your own experience, education and talents) is to 'skill-match'. Considering the job opening, what are the skills needed?

Make a list of the requisite skills (in priority order) and then list concrete examples of your possession of the skill.

For example: a sales representative would need good interpersonal skills, the ability to deal with difficult people. For 'proof' of this skill, you could list experiences and examples of how you were *successful* in a difficult situation.

These matched skills are your *key selling points*.

Next, what appears to be the current problems at the organization, based upon your research? What are their needs that you can meet?

In other words, given the specifics of the company, what value can you add?

After these two steps, you are in a great position to come up with concrete examples of what you can offer the company.

This question, by the way, is just another version of "Why should we hire you?".

In the interview, when asked this question, you could respond with: "In my experience in sales, I know having the ability to deal effectively with all types of people is not merely a positive element --- it is an essential one.

With your plans to expand into ___ market, a sales representative with a proven ability to meet with all types of people and to be able to assess and meet their immediate needs would be a great asset.

In the past __ years, I have increased sales __....."]

THE NEXT FEW QUESTIONS REFER TO YOUR CAREER.

Just to be clear, a *career* refers to different jobs or positions that you have taken within a specific field.

As an example, I'm a Registered Nurse and presumably would be looking for other positions within the healthcare field, specifically nursing.

I could very well change my career and go into something completely different than nursing. Many people do so.

I'm just going to go over them quickly as they seem to be fairly straight forward.

1. Where do you want to be 5 years from now in your career?

2. What are your long-term career goals?

3. What prompted you to take your current job?

4. Where do you see yourself 10 years from now?

5. Why did you make a career change?

6. Why do you want to leave your current position?

7. Five years ago, where did you see yourself today?

8. What is your career goal?

All of these questions are asking you to illustrate that you actually have given some thought to our career path.

Your answer should show that you have. Its not just a matter of job jumping, you need to be able to illustrate that you have a life-long career plan in place.

In the next chapter, we look at interview questions that assess your analytic skills.

6. QUESTIONS TO ASSESS YOUR ANALYTIC SKILLS

These next questions relate to the Interviewer assessing your analytic skills.

If you are applying for a job that relies on their worker's technical and problem-solving skills, you will need to be prepared for these types of questions.

1. Are you analytical? Give us one example of your analytical abilities.

2. Tell us about your analytical skills.

3. Tell us about a particularly difficult problem that you analyzed and what was your recommendation.

4. What steps do you take when analyzing complex problems?

5. How would you rate your analytical ability? Why?

6. How would your manager rate your analytical ability?

If you have recent performance appraisal results, this would be a good place to use your supervisor's exact words.

7. Tell us about a situation where the analysis that you performed was incorrect. What would you have done differently?

This is another version of a question asked earlier where you were asked to come up with a situation that didn't go well and how you turned it around.

8. What do you know about our company?

* [Do you know the company's products/services, mission statement, headquarters location, and name of the CEO?

If not, do a 5-minute internet search on the company.

If you have this information, take the time to look up Interviewer(s) on LinkedIn and notice where they went to school and their history with the company.

(**Hint:** interviewers often like to reflect on their educational experience. Knowing where they went to school can be helpful.)]

OUR NEXT CHAPTER FOCUSES ON COMMUNICATION SKILLS QUESTIONS.

7. QUESTIONS TO ASSESS YOUR COMMUNICATION SKILLS

This chapter focuses on questions that help the Interviewer *assess* your *communication* skills.

Communication skills fit into the category of *soft skills* and some may tell you that they are every bit as important as your *hard* skills.

After-all, if you aren't able to get along with your co-workers and supervisors, you likely aren't a good hire.

I'm just going to list them and wait to comment at the end.

1. **How do you effectively communicate with others?**
2. **How important is listening to effective communications?**
3. **What are some of the characteristics of a good listener?**
4. **Tell us about a situation where you demonstrated good communications skills.**
5. **Tell us about a situation where you demonstrated poor communications skills. What would you have done differently?**
6. **How would you rate your communications skills? Why?**

If you have well-developed communication skills, good for you.

If not, you may want to spend some time researching the topic and seeing if you can develop some specific skills in advance of your interview.

At the very least, learning some new communication skills will help you understand what the Interviewer is looking for in your responses and help you to develop some answers.

Good communication at every level of an organization is important.

You can expect that there will be at least one question on the subject.

Being prepared for these questions may score you some points and answering them well, may illustrate that you do indeed have good communication skills.

Its one thing to say you have them, but answering your questions as efficiently as you can, helps prove the point.

In this next segment, we offer a few questions about communicating with your Co-workers.

1. What are some rules to follow to insure effective communications with your co-workers?

This question would seem to focus on what you consider to be rules.

Hopefully, the Interviewer will see them the same way as you do.

It would be worth your while to determine if there actually are any rules and what they might be.

Think *respect*. Think *assertive communication*.

2. What are some of the means of communication in the workplace?

This question appears to be designed to test your understanding of the communication process.

Your answer should include: 1 to 1 conversations, e-mail 1 to 1 discussions, mass e-mails through distribution lists, written memos on paper, they still exist and don't forget the grapevine.

It exists in every worksite and you will want to be tuned into it.

It wouldn't hurt to offer that gossip also exists, which is a little different than the grapevine and that it has a negative effect in the workplace in many ways.

And you, of course, don't participate in it!

3. **How would your co-workers rate your communications skills?**

You may want to ask some of your co-workers this question. You may not like the answers you get but it would help you to genuinely answer the question.

The secret to answering the question effectively may lay in you sharing what you learned about how your co-workers have commented about your communication skills and what you are doing about it.

IN THE NEXT SEGMENT, WE LOOK AT QUESTIONS RELATED TO communicating with your supervisor.

COMMUNICATING WITH SUPERVISORS:

1. **Communicating with your supervisor is an important aspect of all of our jobs. In addition to being brief, what guidelines should you follow to communicate effectively with your supervisor?**

I would expect that there isn't a definitive answer to this question but some things come to mind from my experience.

- Choose your time. Supervisors can be busy people. Your communication will likely be better received if you speak to them at a time when they are not working on other activities and you have their undivided attention.

- For important discussions that have multiple details, I would suggest sending a follow-up e-mail that outlines the important points that were discussed.

- Clarify the purpose of communicating with your supervisor in advance. Are you informing them of something, are you explaining your role or actions you took in a specific situation, are you asking for their assistance or additional resources, or are you merely updating them, what we call an FYI?

2. **What are the reasons for communicating upwards to your superiors?**

Here are some examples, but once again, develop some of our own.

- Sharing information as to your progress or lack of on a specific topic or project.
- Updating them on any resources that you might need to complete your task.
- Advising them of potential risks or the opposite of sharing with them something that went really well.

3. **How would your supervisor rate your communications skills?**

They're likely looking for something more than a "good!" as an answer to this question.

If your communication skills are good and you have evidence from a performance appraisal validating that a supervisor has said that they are good, you may want to prepare to paraphrase what was said to your benefit.

If your communication skills *aren't* up to snuff and it has been recognized by a supervisor that they need improvement, you can likely turn this to your favour by *admitting* that they aren't as good as they should be *however*, you are *actively* working on steps to improve them.

4. How do you like to be managed/ supervised?

* [The employer is really asking *how much* supervision you need. Be honest, but understand employers select candidates who *know* when to ask questions and *when* to work independently.]

This next segment offers some suggestions for questions that may be asked if you are applying for a supervisory position.

If you are not applying for a supervisory position, you may want to move forward in the program to the next chapter.

These following questions are testing your knowledge of the supervisory process.

If you have supervisory experience to draw from, you will want to provide some answers based on your experience.

5. How can a supervisor establish effective communications with staff?

Some supervisors feel that an open-door policy is best. This is where the employees are told that your door is open all the time and they should feel free to come to you to talk about their problems.

The downside, for supervisors that have a tendency to micro-manage, is that it can create a culture where the employees get used to running to the boss to solve all problems.

It can also create a situation where individual employees are competing for attention from the supervisor and use dysfunctional interpersonal communication techniques to meet their needs.

On, the other hand, an open-door policy can foster good communications with your workers if you set up your expectations in the first place.

Some examples might be ... if you have a problem with a co-worker, talk to them first to try to resolve the issue. If you are unable to resolve it, then come to me.

You could encourage a 'no-gossip' policy. If you are coming to complain about another and you haven't tried to resolve it, well then go back to them and try.

Don't accept unilateral complaining from employees about other employees.

6. What means of communication may be used to effectively establish a new policy?

Over my career, I have been involved in all aspects of policy and procedures.

When I was in my younger rebel years, I found that many policies & procedures were created to control me or stop me from doing something I shouldn't have been doing.

The simplest way to establish a new policy in the workplace is to post it to a Policy & Procedure Manual with the expectation that all employees will read it.

Simple yes, effective no.

In most cases, it would be more effective to discuss the new policy with those that it effects at a staff meeting.

Employees need to know the importance of the policy, assuming that there really is importance.

Everyone needs to know that the policy exists and the purpose that it was designed for.

7. Are there additional considerations in communicating to groups of employees versus individual employees?

A wise rule of thumb is to *praise* in public and to *criticize* in private.

Too bad many supervisors don't know about it or choose not to.

8. What are some good rules to keep in mind when directing employees?

Here are some examples. You should be prepared to supply your own.

- Your expectations should be clearly outlined.
- What is the desired end result of the employee completing a task?
- Are you delegating any responsibility or authority to the specific employee?
- Are there any time constraints involved?
- That is, are you expecting partial or complete results by a certain time?

9. In what instances, is written communication better than verbal communications?

In an employee contract or work agreement, the terms of employment would be helpful.

Another example relates to employee performance standards, where a Letter of Expectation might be issued to the employee from the Employer, outlining that performance expectations have not been met and the consequences should the expectations not be met by a certain date.

Yet another example would be the organization's policy and procedure manual that specifically outlines situations and actions that the employee would need as a reference rather than going by memory of an oral conversation

IN THE NEXT CHAPTER, WE LOOK AT DECISION MAKING QUESTIONS.

8. DECISION MAKING PROCESS QUESTIONS

This chapter looks at questions that assess your *decision-making* processes.

1. What type of decisions do you make in your current position?

Every position has elements of it that require you to make decisions, whether they be minor ones or those that have a greater impact.

Choose some examples where your decisions have had a positive response and focus you in a favourable light.

2. What decisions are easiest for you to make and which ones are the most difficult? Why?

* [In addressing the decisions that are the most difficult for you, don't cite decisions that are essential to the job that you are interviewing for.

For the decisions that you do cite, expand your answer by telling what steps that you're taking to improve your decision making.]

3. What steps are involved in making a decision?

This question may be a little more complicated than it seems. The interviewer is testing your decision-making processes.

You may want to do some research on this topic to be prepared.

Something to think about is that many decisions are based on one's logical thoughts vs their emotional ones. In sales, many purchases are made on emotion, but justified by logic.

Many people use a pro vs con approach. What happens if I take this approach, what happens if I don't.

4. What items of information do *you* typically need before you make a decision?

Remember, there are no perfect decisions and in many situations, you will never have all the facts.

This question seems to be asking about your decision-making process so you will need to provide specifics, rather than generalities.

5. Give us an example of your ability to make decisions under pressure.

Once again, you are being assessed. So, provide an example or two with favourable results and that make you look good.

6. Tell us about the worst decision that you've made on the job.

Be careful with this one!

You want to make it look like you are capable of learning from bad decisions and not that you regularly make bad decisions.

7. Tell us about the best decision that you've made on the job.

Here is another opportunity for shining.

8. How would you rate a job that requires you to constantly make decisions?

I'm not really sure what is being asked here.

I would suspect that they are really asking 'how would you do working in our job that requires you to constantly make decisions?"

OUR NEXT CHAPTER LOOKS AT WHAT OTHERS WOULD SAY ABOUT YOU.

9. 'WHAT WOULD DIFFERENT PEOPLE SAY ABOUT YOU?' TYPE QUESTIONS

This chapter addresses what you expect different people would say about you, if they were asked. In this area of questioning you are likely better to appear *humble*, yet *self-confident*.

These following three questions can likely be answered well by referring to any recent performance appraisals.

That way you are using your supervisor's own words for your answer.

1. What do you think your supervisor would say about your work?

2. What do you think your co-worker would say about your work?

3. What would your boss say about you - both positive and negative?

4. What would your subordinates say about - both positive and negative?

This question presumes that you have other employees that you oversee various aspects of their job performance.

This can be a challenging question to answer in that most of the time, we don't ask our subordinates what they think of us. Perhaps we are probably better off not knowing.

5. What would your co-workers say about you - both positive and negative?

It can be easy to respond to the positive thoughts that our co-workers think but not so the negative.

Unless you are a mind-reader, this question can be difficult to answer. You may get by with acknowledging you aren't a mind-reader but then provide some examples of how you sense people respond to you.

It is a fact that not everybody in the world will get along with you, so if you do have some that you don't get along with, it *won't* necessarily work against you.

6. What three keywords would your peers use to describe you?

This is a challenging question. If you don't know, go ahead and ask them.

You will likely get different answers from everyone, so see if there are any themes that come up consider them and choose three of them.

7. What one thing would your boss say that he or she has the greatest problem with you?

Hopefully, you will never be asked this question.

Choose something benign.

I once had a manager say in a performance appraisal that the only negative thing she had to say about me was that she wished she had more time to spend with me.

I've always taken is as she enjoyed her time with me.

Now that I think about it ... I'm hoping that she didn't mean that I needed a lot of help from her.

Hmm. No, I don't think so!

8. Describe a situation in which your work was criticized?

Describe the situation and how you responded to the criticism.

This question refers to your work being *criticized* rather than you receiving *constructive feedback*.

Likely, most people respond to criticism in the way that it was delivered to them.

Criticism is *negative* in nature. Some believe that *launching* a counter-attack can be a good defence.

In this case a good answer would include you accepting the criticism, accepting it in the sense that you *agree* to consider its merit.

Then you would ask the criticizer to back up the points they have made with examples. If generalizations have been made, you could point out the inaccuracies.

A productive way of dealing with unfair criticism includes you taking an *assertive* approach to challenging the individual who has criticized you.

Just *because* they have said something about you, doesn't *necessarily* make it *true*.

If you haven't responded effectively to criticism in the past, you can probably turn it to your advantage in the interview question by *briefly* describing a situation that you didn't handle well but explain that you have *learned* how to deal with it assertively and will handle it differently in the future.

This could be an example of the Past, Present and Future model for answering a question that we talked about a few chapters back.

You are in essence, turning a negative into a positive example that will help make you look better.

9. How would your subordinates describe you?

This is a different version of a question we looked at earlier.

10 **Tell us about the last time you lost your temper?**

11. **What situations *make* you lose your temper?**

If you're not a person that loses their temper, say so.

If you *are*, be *careful* with your response.

Losing one's temper is often related to *not having* the skills to solve a particular problem.

The Interviewer is testing your ability to problem solve and remain in control of yourself with the situation you find yourself in.

12. **Tell us about the worst supervisor you've worked under.**

This can be a loaded question.

You will need to provide examples of why they were the worst and how you were able to work with them or not.

13. **Tell us about the *best* supervisor you've worked under.**

Given this question you could highlight the supervisor's positive attributes that you have liked.

Actions such as they were a good teacher or mentor would be helpful.

14. **Tell us about a confrontation that you've had with a co-worker.**

The important part of responding to this question would be in sharing how you successfully resolved the confrontation and moved forward in working together.

15. **How do you maintain an effective working relationship with your coworkers?**

This is an interesting question as it is assessing your working skills.

Getting along with your co-workers is important. Certainly, for you, but perhaps even more for your manager.

They don't want to be spending all their time intervening in employee interpersonal conflict. It takes away from more important work that they should be doing.

16. How would your best friend describe you?

This one should be fairly easy to answer. I would expect that you have many things in common and hopefully your best friend is supportive of you.

If not, maybe it's time to get a new best friend.

17. How would your worst enemy describe you?

I would suggest staying fairly neutral and reply that you don't believe or are aware that you have any enemies, let alone a worst enemy.

Admitting that you do could lead you to follow-up questions that you wouldn't want to answer and certainly wouldn't make you look good.

In our next chapter, we look at Strengths vs Weaknesses Interview Questions.

10. STRENGTHS VS WEAKNESSES INTERVIEW QUESTIONS

There are *many* questions that an Interviewer can ask you about your strengths.

I've commented on a few of them, but the *main* concept is that you share your responses in a *thoughtful* manner that highlights you well, but not at the expense of someone else.

1. Why should we hire you?

Be careful with your answer here.

It isn't a time to be flippant. Saying "That you'd be stupid not to!" won't help you.

However, this is a good time to remind the interviewer what you do have to offer.

2. What are your three greatest strengths?

Your response to this should tie in with your Summary Statement from your resume.

It's another chance to reinforce what you have to offer.

3. What can you contribute to our organization?

This is where having a good understanding of the organization's history and culture would come in.

You could align yourself with a cause that they believe in.

4. Assume that you are a candidate in the coming general election. Tell me why you are the best candidate in the field.

Let's hope you don't get asked this one, unless you actually are applying for a position within a political party.

This question is likely asking several things beneath the surface. How confident are you? Can you be self-promoting yet humble at the same time?

It also addresses how you speak about the competition.

Here's some more examples of strength type questions:

5. What is your greatest strength?

6. We've interviewed a number of highly qualified students for this position. What sets you apart from the others?

7. What are your strengths?

8. Select four to five strengths that are *job-related*, highlighting technical and leadership skills and work ethic.

9. What part of your current job are you the most comfortable with?

Presumably, your *strengths* are what helps you become comfortable with a specific aspect of your *current* job.

Think of some examples that highlight your strengths. Perhaps you are good at customer service and working with people. Not everybody is.

Some people are more comfortable working with numbers. If that is your case, find a way to highlight the fact.

10. What are your strong points and how have they helped you to succeed?

~

IN THIS NEXT SEGMENT, WE LOOK AT QUESTIONS THAT ADDRESS YOUR *weaknesses*.

You shouldn't feel intimidated about these questions.

We all have weaknesses.

Fortunately, we all have different weaknesses.

What really matters is that you have *acknowledged* that you aren't as strong in an area as you could be and that you are working on *improving* your skills and confidence in the area.

What ever you come up with for an answer, you should probably find a way to tie it into the job position you are applying for.

Not the fact that you are weak in the area but perhaps your willingness to *strengthen* your level of competency for the benefit of yourself and your new employer.

Here's a few personal weakness type questions.

They are all really variations on the same question.

1. What is your greatest weakness?

* [Mention one work-related challenge that you are prepared to overcome. For example: I know there will be a learning curve before I am as productive as you would like a top performing (name of job you are applying for) to be. I have always been able to master the skills necessary to be successful, and I am confident I can do that working for (name of company).]

2. Name your three greatest weaknesses.

3. Which is the worst of your three greatest weaknesses and why?

4. What are your weaknesses?

And here's some more ...

5. What part of your current job are you the least comfortable with?

6. What are your weak points and how have you overcome them?

7. What about yourself would you want to improve?

8. In which area do you need to make the improvement in?

IN THE NEXT CHAPTER, WE LOOK AT QUESTIONS THAT ARE SPECIFIC TO interviewing for supervisory positions.

If you aren't applying for a supervisor's position, skip forward to the next chapter in this section.

11. SUPERVISOR ROLE SPECIFIC QUESTIONS

The questions in this chapter, apply to job searchers who are applying for a supervisory position.

I'm not going to go into detail with these questions as they *likely* apply to a smaller group of job searchers than the general ones.

The questions are fairly specific, so you may want to spend some time on your own researching and developing some appropriate responses.

If you aren't applying for a supervisory position, please move on to the next chapter.

1. What is the purpose of a performance appraisal?

2. What is the most important quality a supervisor should have?

3. An employee approaches you with a sexual harassment-related problem. In your discussion with the employee, what items of information will be of the most importance?

4. What are the characteristics of an effective supervisor?

5. What qualities make for a good boss?

6. What steps can a supervisor take to improve the capabilities of staff?

7. How should an assignment be made to an employee?

8. How would a supervisor evaluate an administrative employee's performance?

9. What are the three most common weaknesses of managers and supervisors?

10. Why is feedback important?

11. What are some of the ways in which an employee starts to behave that usually indicate a potential problem?

12. What guidelines should be followed in counselling an employee?

13. Name the major sources of conflict in organizations.

14. Describe the process by which conflict in an organization should be addressed.

15. What are the five functions of a supervisor?

16. What considerations should be made in establishing organizational goals for your unit?

17. What actions can a supervisor take to insure that subordinates support the mission and goals of an organization?

18. Vacations during the holidays are popular among employees. Describe the actions a supervisor can take to insure that service levels are unaffected during these times.

19. What are guidelines to follow in constructively criticizing an employee?

20. What are some of the signs that your staff may be suffering from burnout?

[Declining health, increasing sickness and tardiness, absentmindedness, flaring tempers and procrastination.]

In the next chapter, we look at get to know you type questions.

12. PERSONAL 'GET TO KNOW YOU' TYPE INTERVIEW QUESTIONS

This chapter deals with personal 'get to know you' type interview questions.

As you would suspect, there are no right or wrong answers to these ones.

The purpose would seem to be for the Interviewer to take a *reading* on you as a person, separate from your work life. This would be *subjective* on their part of course.

For responding to these questions, you will want to be *upbeat, positive-thinking* and as always ... show yourself in a good light.

Be careful of what some of us call *TMI* ... too much information. You don't want to provide so much information that the Interviewer will start thinking about follow-up questions to what you have provided.

"Why in the world did you ever do that?" comes to mind.

I'm just going to list them and you can develop your own answers.

1. **Tell us about the passion in your life as it relates to your work.**

2. **What aspects of your work do you get the most excited about?**

3. What are your most outstanding qualities?

4. If you were to start your own company, what would that company do?

5. Tell me about the last book that you read.

6. If you were a cucumber in a salad and somebody was about to eat you, what would you do?

This has to be one of the stupidest interview questions I've heard.

But you need to be prepared for questions that seem to come from outer space.

7. What are your worst qualities?

It might be a good opportunity to say that you don't taste very good in a salad in regards to the previous question, but you may want avoid it.

8. What is your favourite colour and what does it reflect in your personality?

9. Rate yourself from one to ten on your work ethic with ten being the best.

10. Describe yourself.

11. How would your friends describe you?

12. Do you like to socialize outside of work?

13. What are your hobbies?

IN THE NEXT CHAPTER, WE LOOK AT ILLEGAL INTERVIEW QUESTIONS AND how to answer them, or not!

13. ILLEGAL INTERVIEW QUESTIONS

Interviewing job applicants has likely been with us *forever*.

Over the past 40 years or so with the development of human rights, there has been development in the area of what *kinds* of questions and *specific* questions that Interviewers are able to ask you.

It can vary from country to country, so you would be *well advised* to do your own research to find out how things stand in your country.

These samples are provided for illustrative purpose only ... drawn from Canadian and American resources and should not be considered as facts in law.

If you are interested in furthering your knowledge of questions that are appropriate vs illegal I would suggest that you research the Human Rights Commission in the province or state that you live in.

What can you do if you are asked an illegal question?

If you're asked an illegal question you have several options available to you.

You can choose to answer the question and that is well within your rights, but you can also refuse to answer as well.

Of course, taking this option may possibly create a rift between you and the Interviewer.

However, if you choose to answer an illegal question, remember that you are giving information that isn't related to the job; in fact, you might be giving the "wrong" answer, which could harm your chances of getting the job.

You can *refuse* to answer the question, which is well within your rights.

Unfortunately, depending on how you phrase your refusal, you run the *risk* of coming off as *uncooperative* or *confrontational* - hardly words an employer would use to describe the *"ideal"* candidate.

You can examine the question for its *intent* and *respond* with an answer as it might apply to the job.

For example, the Interviewer asks, "Are you a Canadian/US citizen?" or "What country are you from?"

You've been asked an illegal question.

You could respond, however, with "I am *authorized* to work in the USA." [or whatever country you live in]

Similarly, let's say the Interviewer asks, "Who is going to take care of your children when you have to travel for the job?"

You might answer, "I can *meet* the *travel* and *work* schedule that this job requires."

If you can't see the *intent* behind the question, then ask "Can you tell me how this relates to my ability to fill the position?"

Most (if not all) interviewers will reword the question as it *relates* to the position.

You can also *choose to inform* the Interviewer that the question they asked is illegal.

It's entirely possible that the Interviewer was not aware of this fact or they may have just awkwardly phrased a *perfectly* legal question.

There is also the chance that calling out a potential employer might make the interview process go worse, but you may not want to work for an organization that bases employment on inappropriate questions.

Please locate the Handout entitled ***Interview Questions – Legal vs Illegal*** located in the Resources Section at the end of the book for more detail.

It addresses specific areas of questioning that are illegal to ask and how it could or should be asked.

We won't be discussing it here.

In the next chapter we introduce a technique of handling behavioural based questions.

14. BE A STAR!

Job interviewing techniques have continued to evolve over the years.

In earlier chapters, we have looked at several different ways to answer interview questions and looked at some *specific* questions you might be asked.

We are now going to build upon those techniques with yet another one. That is, being prepared to be a ***STAR***.

STAR is an interview response technique that can be used by job seekers.

The STAR interview response technique is a method for answering behavioural interview questions. Behavioural interview questions are questions about how you have behaved in the past.

Specifically, they are about how you have handled certain work situations.

Interviewers ask these questions to see if candidates have the skills and experiences required for the job. One good way for them to see if candidates have what it takes is to look at past examples of performance.

Competency questions make up a large part of most job interviews and from a company's point of view they allow an objective assessment of a candidate's experience and the qualities that make them suitable for the job.

The STAR technique of interviewing makes it easier for the employer to compare all the people who are applying for the job in a methodical and structured way.

Here are some examples of behavioural interview questions. We will look at more examples later on:

- Tell me about a time you had to complete a task under a tight deadline.
- Have you ever gone above and beyond the call of duty?
- What do you do when a team member refuses to complete his or her portion of the work?

By now you are probably wondering what STAR stands for?

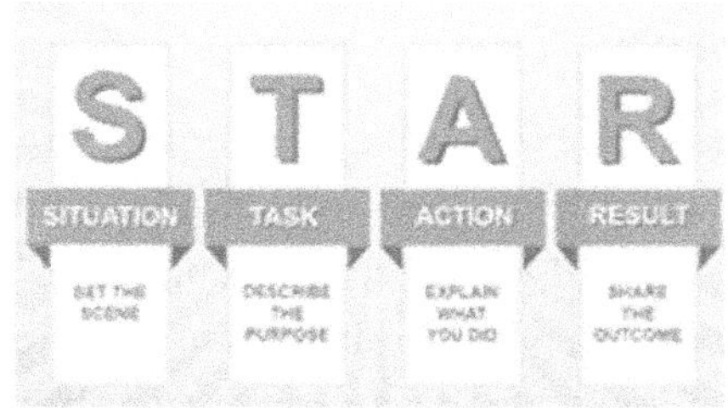

STAR IS AN ACRONYM FOR FOUR KEY CONCEPTS.

Each concept is a step the job candidate can take to answer a behavioural interview question.

By completing all four steps, the job candidate provides a thorough answer.

The concepts in the acronym include:

Situation: Describe a situation or problem that you have encountered.

Task: Describe the task that the situation required or your ideas for resolving the problem.

Action: Describe the action you took, obstacles that you had to overcome.

Results: Highlight outcomes achieved.

We'll expand upon each of these steps in a moment.

Which questions need a STAR response?

The questions will usually start along the lines of "tell me about a time when you".

This will be followed by those competencies that have been listed on the job specification, so it is important to be familiar with these so that you can prepare.

For example, a marketing executive may require problem-solving skills, or a job in customer services may require conflict management skills. That would mean if you were applying for those jobs you would be well-advised to prepare answers to questions designed to determine whether you have the competency or not.

Hopefully you do!

Some interviewers structure their questions using the STAR technique. You may encounter a series of questions based around assessing one competency.

Here's a quick example: "Tell me about a time you had to complete a task under a tight deadline. Describe the situation, and explain how you handled it."

Since you won't know in advance what interviewing techniques your Interviewer will be using, you'll benefit from preparing several scenarios from the jobs you've held.

First, make a list of the skills and/or experiences required for the job. You might look at the job listing for suggestions. Then, consider specific examples of times that you displayed those skills.

For each example, name the ***situation, task, action, and result.***

You can also look at common behavioural interview questions and try answering each of them using the ***STAR*** technique.

We'll provide a list of behavioural interview questions for you to practice on a little later.

Whatever examples you select, make sure they are as closely related to the job you're interviewing for as possible. Now, let's break the steps down into greater detail.

Situation:

This is about setting the scene, giving a context and background to the situation. This situation can be from a work experience, a volunteer position, or any other relevant event.

Be as specific as possible.

You must describe a specific event or situation, not a generalized description of what you have done in the past. Be sure to give enough detail for the interviewer to understand.

Describe the context within which you performed a job or faced a challenge at work. Make it *concise and informative*, concentrating solely on what is useful to the story.

For example, perhaps you were working on a group project, or you had a conflict with a co-worker.

So, if you're asked a question about time management, your reply would need to include the details of the project you were working on, who you were working with, when it happened and where you were.

As another example, if the question is asking you to describe a situation where you had to deal with a difficult person, explain how you came to meet that person and why they were being difficult.

If the question is asking for an example of teamwork, explain the task that you had to undertake as a team.

Task

This is more *specific* to your exact role in the situation you are providing, so describe your responsibility in that situation.

You need to make sure that the interviewer knows what you were tasked with, rather than the rest of the team.

Examples: Perhaps you had to help your group complete a project under a tight deadline, or resolve a conflict with a co-worker.

Another ... "It was my responsibility to find an alternative so it didn't reflect badly on the company and we didn't waste the opportunity."

Action: This is the most important section of the STAR approach as it is where you will need to demonstrate and highlight the skills and personal attributes that the question is testing i.e. what your response to the situation was.

Remember, you need to talk about what you specifically did, so using 'I' rather than team actions – otherwise you won't be showing off the necessary skills the employer is looking for.

Be sure to share a lot of detail, the interviewer will not be familiar with your history, although remember to avoid any acronyms and institutional language.

Now that you have set the situation of your story, you need to explain what you did.

In doing so, you will need to remember the following:

- Be personal, i.e. talk about you, not the rest of the team.
- Go into some detail.
- Do not assume that they will guess what you mean.
- Avoid technical information, unless it is crucial to your story.
- Don't tell what you might do, explain what you did, how you did it, and why you did it.

What you're trying to get across here is how you assessed and decided what was the appropriate response to the situation and how you got the other team members involved – which in turn is a great way to demonstrate your communication skills.

What you did and how you did it.

The interviewers will want to know how you reacted to the situation.

This is where you can start selling some important skills that you have.

For example, you may want to describe how you used the team to achieve a particular objective and how you used your communication skills to keep everyone updated on progress etc.

Here's another example, if you are asked about dealing with a difficult personality on your team you would talk about how you decided to take a certain course of action to avoid making the situation worse or upsetting the individual.

Why you did it.

By highlighting the reasons behind your action, you would make a greater impact.

For example; when discussing a situation where you had to deal with conflict, many candidates would simply say: "I told my colleague to calm down and explained to him what the problem was."

However, it would not provide a good idea of what drove you to act in this manner.

How did you ask him to calm down?

How did you explain the nature of the problem?

Here's an example of what you could say:

"I could sense that my colleague was irritated and I asked him gently to tell me what he felt the problem was.

By allowing him to express his feelings and his anger, I gave him the opportunity to calm down. I then explained to him my own point of view on the matter, emphasizing how important it was that we found a solution that suited us both."

This revised answer helps the interviewers understand what drove your actions and reinforces the feeling that you are calculating the consequences of your actions, thus retaining full control of the situation.

It provides much more information about you as an individual and is another reason why the STAR approach is so useful.

Result: Finally, explain the outcomes or results generated by the action taken. You might emphasize what you accomplished, or what you learned.

The result should be a positive one, and ideally one that can be quantified. Numbers always impress employers.

Think back to CAR/SAR statements that we talked about in Section I, Part Two, Chapter 7, in regards to resumes.

Examples of quantification, include repeat business, an increase in sales by 15% or saving the team 5 hours a week.

The Interviewer will also want to know what you learnt from the situation and if there was anything you'd do differently the next time you were faced a similar situation.

Here's an example, "Joseph didn't make the meeting on time but we explained the problem to the 30 delegates and Frederick's presentation went well – a bit rough around the edges but it was warmly received.

Joseph managed to get there for the last 20 minutes to answer questions.

As a result, we gained some good contacts, at least two of which we converted into paying clients."

There are a few things to note with this response: it's important to speak in *specific* rather than *general* terms and *quantify* your success.

In this example, we mentioned 30 delegates, the names of the people involved and quantified two contacts converted to clients.

From a *listener's* perspective, this makes the story more interesting and they are more able to gauge your success.

Nameless figures and *undefined* successes can make the answer less feel less convincing.

Secondly, as there are likely to be many questions and interviewers have short attention spans, it's important to keep your answers concise: convey the maximum achievement in the minimum time.

Finally, it's important to finish on a positive note so the overall impression is strong.

For a longer list of these types of questions, view the Behavioural-Competency Based Interview Questions Handout, in the Resources Section.

In the next chapter we look at common job searching mistakes and how to prevent them.

15. COMMON JOB SEARCHING MISTAKES & PREVENTION

In this chapter, we provide examples of common job interview mistakes and how to *prevent* them from *happening* in the first place.

At any given time, there are *countless* people who are looking for employment.

As we have advocated throughout this program, there are *right ways and wrong ways* to go about your job search. Yet so many people are still doing things that *hurt* their chances of finding employment.

You don't want to rub prospective employers the *wrong* way. After all, competition for jobs can be extremely *competitive*. Why reduce your chances of being selected as a successful candidate?

To help you put forth your best impression possible, here are some examples of job interview mistakes that others have made. If *you* don't make them in the *first* place, you won't have to worry about how to correct them.

Common Job Interview Mistakes

- **When contacted for an interview, the applicant says they have no idea who the person calling is and asks what job this is.**

Ok, maybe in some extreme cases the applicant may have *forgotten* applying for the position. However, you should always pay attention to the job postings that you apply for.

Make sure that you keep a file of all the job advertisements you apply for as well as the cover letter you write for it (remember each job should get its own cover letter written specifically to the job requirements of that position and how you meet those requirements.)

Do some research on the company you are applying to and research what the position is so that you are well-aware of the company or the position when you get a call for an interview.

- **The candidate shows up late for the interview.**

Being late for an interview? Really?

Things do happen but by all means give yourself enough time to arrive a little early for your interview.

First impressions are huge.

If you can't show up on time for the interview, how can the employer count on you, day to day in the job? No excuse (traffic back up, road construction, got lost, etc.) is going to change the poor first impression you've made.

Leave extra early to allow for any delays be ready to interview when you walk in the door. Map out your route on your phone so that you know exactly where to go, what floor to go to and which person to ask for.

- **The candidate shows up too early.**

On the flip-side, avoid showing up for the interview too early.

Why is this a problem?

Quite often interviews are scheduled back to back and it is awkward for the Receptionist to have 2 or 3 people waiting for interviews. As well if you are the first interview of the day the office may not be ready for you yet.

It is best that you do arrive to the area early but only come into the building 5-10 minutes early prior to your interview.

- **The applicant brings too many items with them to the interview.**

Nothing is more distracting, unprofessional and disorganized than when you arrive juggling your cell phone, a Starbucks or Tim Hortons coffee cup, a huge purse/backpack/briefcase, an umbrella and a coat!

Be prepared and arrive with only the essentials that you need to participate in the interview.

Ideally, you will want to arrive with only your car keys, your phone (more on that in a second) and a small folder or briefcase (that contains your resume, references, cover letter, the job advertisement, company information and some questions that you may have about the company or position).

Leave all unnecessary baggage hidden in your vehicle and arrive composed and ready to participate in your interview.

- **The applicant is texting or on the phone.**

We get it, we are a plugged-in world, but by all means, ignore your phone for 30-60 minutes when you are in your interview.

Turn it off, ensure that your ringer is off and maybe better yet leave your phone in your purse, backpack or briefcase. There is nothing more annoying that your phone ringing or buzzing during a meeting… interviews are no exception.

Shut off your cell phone before you get to the interview.

- **The candidate is chewing gum, candy or carrying a coffee.**

This is very unprofessional and far too casual behaviour. Spit out your gum into a garbage can before you get to the building and get a coffee after the interview.

If you are offered a beverage during the interview, by all means accept it, but don't bring your own.

- **Candidate wears strong perfume/cologne/scents or smokes right before the interview.**

You want to be conscious of how many people have allergies to scents or asthma sensitivities.

You also want to make a great first impression and sending the receptionist or Interviewer into an allergic reaction is not going to help.

For you smokers out there, while you may not be able to smell the smoke and nicotine emanating from your person, others can. Try to avoid lighting up before an interview.

- **Research the parking situation.**

Prior to arriving be sure to know where you can park and if you need to pay for parking. Make sure you plug the parking meter sufficiently. Have an idea of how long your interview is expected to take and put more money in the meter than you need.

You don't want to have to interrupt the interview to go plug the parking meter, so be prepared ahead of time.

- **Applicant dresses inappropriately.**

Depending on the type of job being applied for, your attire may vary. Regardless, you should dress professionally without overdressing for your interview.

Mini-skirts, impractical high heels, or casual, immodest or flashy clothing will set the wrong impression. For any professional position, erring on the side of modest will always help make the right impression.

If you are serious about finding a good job for yourself, you will take each chance you need to make an excellent impression. Applicants lose the interest of employers if they are unprofessional or casual.

- **Candidate talks too much.**

Interviews should involve two-way dialogue.

While the *employer* is looking to learn more about you, avoid *dominating* the conversation and not letting the Interviewer get a word in. Listen *carefully* and provide a *clear concise* response to questions.

Use your judgement as to when you need to communicate additional details.

Being confident is one thing but being a chatty pants can be annoying and may impact the first impression that you are presenting.

- **Fuzzy Resume Facts**

Even if you have submitted a resume when you applied for the job, you may also be asked to fill out a job application during your interview.

Make sure you know the information you will need to complete an application including dates of prior employment, graduation dates and employer contact information. It's understandable that some of your older experiences may be hard to recall.

Review the facts before your interview. It can be helpful to keep a copy of your resume for yourself to refer to during your interview, although certainly don't use it as a crutch.

- **Not Paying Attention**

Don't let yourself zone out during an interview. Make sure you are well-rested, alert and prepared for your interview.

Getting distracted and missing a question looks bad on your part. If you zone out, your potential employer will wonder how you will be able to stay focused during a day on the job, if you can't even focus during one interview.

If you feel your attention slipping away, make the effort to stay engaged. Maintain eye contact, lean forward slightly when talking to your Interviewer and make an active effort to listen effectively.

While you may have no problem paying attention in a one-on-one interview in a private office, it's harder to stay in tune with the interviewer when you're meeting in a public place.

- **Not Being Prepared to Answer Questions**

Your Interviewer is probably going to ask you more than just the basics about where you worked, and when.

To get a feel of your aptitude for a job, your Interviewer is going to take advantage of the allotted time and flesh out everything he or she needs to know about you as an employee.

Don't let yourself be caught off guard. Prepare for your interview by reviewing what questions to expect, and how to answer them.

Be prepared with a list of questions to ask the employer so you're ready when you asked if you have questions for the Interviewer.

- **Not having any questions**

Most Interviewers leave time at the end to answer questions. Usually, they know you're vetting them, too, and want to make sure it's a two-sided conversation.

It's also a bit of a test.

The questions you ask often reveal the way you think and what's important to you. It also shows that you care enough about the job that you want to know more.

Not having any questions prepared, signals you don't care, aren't curious, or haven't done your homework.

If you freeze up, throw out an old standby question like, "What does success look like in this role?" or "What's the culture like here?"

- **Asking weirdly personal questions**

Conversely, some candidates get a little too personal with their questions.

Your questions should be related to the job in discussion, not related to the interviewer.

- **Badmouthing Past Employers**

Don't make the mistake of badmouthing your boss or coworkers.

It's sometimes a smaller world than you think and you don't know who your Interviewer might know, including that boss who is an idiot...

You also don't want the Interviewer to think that you might speak that way about his or her company if you leave on terms that aren't the best.

When interviewing for a job, you want your employer to know that you can work well with other people and handle conflicts in a mature and effective way, rather than badmouthing your coworkers or talking about other's incompetence.

When you're asked hard questions, like "Tell me about a time that you didn't work well with a supervisor. What was the outcome and how would you have changed the outcome?"

Or "Have you worked with someone you didn't like? If so, how did you handle it?," don't fall back on badmouthing other people. Instead, review how to answer difficult questions.

- **Displaying low energy**

This one is hard to define but an interview killer.

Here's what it looks like: Slumped shoulders, lack of eye contact, slowness to respond to questions and a general lack of enthusiasm for the company or role.

If you don't clearly want the job, it's near impossible to persuade someone to give it to you.

- **Focusing too much on themselves**

Talking endlessly about what you want, how this job is the direction you want to go in your career and how the experience would be great for you is meaningless drivel to an Interviewer.

Companies don't pay you to help you out!

They hire you because you have traits and skills that will help them achieve their goals. Use your responses to illustrate how you can be of service to the hiring manager.

- **Forgetting to follow up**

So many people forget this basic rule of interviewing: Follow up within 24 hours by email to thank the Interviewer for their time and underscore your interest in the position.

If you don't do it, hiring managers may think you're not interested or organized, or they may simply forget about you.

- **Following up too aggressively**

While it's important to follow up, you should not send multiple emails or call an Interviewer.

It is extremely awkward for Employers to receive a call out of the blue from someone demanding to know why they haven't heard from them.

Send your follow-up email, and then move on with your life. Anything more is probably too much.

- **Being angry**

Angry people are NOT people employers want to hire.

Angry people are not fun to work with. They may frighten co-workers and/or customers or clients. They may also abuse both people and equipment (computers, cars, etc.).

Instead: If you are angry over a job loss, horrible commute to the interview, earlier fight with your kids or spouse, or anything else, dump the anger before the interview, at least temporarily.

Stop, before you enter the employer's premises, take a few deep breaths, put a smile on your face and do your best to switch gears mentally so you are not "in a bad place" in your mind.

- **Sharing TMI (too much information)**

Sometimes, people have a whole-truth-and-nothing-but-the-truth mindset in a job interview, so they "spill their guts" in answer to every question. Not smart or useful!

We're not recommending telling any lies, but we are recommending that you avoid boring the interviewer and blowing an opportunity by sharing too much information.

If they want more details, they'll ask.

Instead: Answer their question, and then stop talking. Or, ask a question of your own.

- **Negative body language**

If you never smile, have a limp handshake, and don't make eye contact with the people you meet at the employer's location and especially with the Interviewer, you'll come across as too shy or too strange or simply not interested.

Instead: Show your interest and enthusiasm.

- **Flirting or other inappropriate behaviour**

Unless you are interviewing for a job as a comedian or host/hostess in a social club, don't try to be entertaining or amusing.

And, don't flirt with anyone, including the receptionist and the security guard.

Instead: If making them laugh isn't a requirement of the job, take the interview seriously.

Save flirting for your second day of work.

- **Not having an elevator pitch.**

Likely, in every interview, you'll encounter some variation of the "tell me about yourself" prompt.

This is a direct invitation to outshine your resume, tell the employer what value you're bringing to the table, and address any weaknesses or anomalies in your employment or educational record.

Too many people think they'll be able to "wing" this part of the interview, but scientifically, it's just not possible:

The average human attention span is five seconds, so if you aren't ready to go when the moment comes, you'll lose the Interviewer's interest in the time it takes you to craft a response.

This completely defeats the purpose of the elevator pitch, which is to start - not conclude - the conversation.

- **Asking for feedback after being rejected.**

Requesting feedback or suggestions for improvement may demonstrate your humility and dedication to personal growth, but it puts the hiring manager in an awkward position.

Furthermore, it's unlikely that you'll get a straightforward response, because most feedback can create a legal liability for the employer...

Additionally, and perhaps most importantly, responding to requests for feedback takes up time the employer doesn't have, which is often seen as intrusive and irritating.

So, please, reconsider asking for it.

Note: This is another one of those controversial suggestions. Other experts will tell you that you should follow-up with rejections.

You may learn some valuable information for your next interview.

- **Missing Opportunities to Prove Yourself.**

Interviewers will ask questions that give you the chance to demonstrate your qualifications and show you have what it takes to do the job.

"Failure to answer questions with ESR (Example, Specifics, Results) responses," is a failure to make the most of the interview.

Most questions offer you the opportunity in your answer to provide the Interviewer with specific, relevant examples of you accomplishing some type of measurable result that benefited the employer.

This requires you to have done your homework ahead of time and to accurately portray what happened, so that when the employer verifies your story with prior employers, it matches what you said.

- **Begging for the job**

Even if you are desperate for work, begging won't help.

You will likely embarrass your Interviewer and will lower your chances of being considered for the job.

I personally have experienced this when I was hiring to fill a position.

- **Forgetting to notify your references that you have just had an interview and the employer may be calling**

It can be a waste of an Interviewer's time and effort to contact one of your references only to find out that they didn't know that they were a reference or that they didn't know all that much about you.

Securing a job interview should be considered as success, but it is often just the first step in the process.

In order to make a great impression you will want to avoid the job interview mistakes listed above. Be prepared, project confidence and be professional.

A mediocre interview can make or break your chances of a second interview or of receiving an offer.

~

IN OUR NEXT SECTION, SECTION VII, WE TAKE A BRIEF LOOK AT questions to ask an interviewer.

SECTION VII

Questions to Ask an Interviewer

1. QUESTIONS TO ASK AN INTERVIEWER

In this chapter, we'll look at questions that you can, should and probably shouldn't ask your interviewer.

Let's get started.

It's worth repeating ... **Will Rogers** said, "I never met a man I didn't like."

An employment interview is a place to be *liked*. Unless you're *likeable*, you won't be *hireable*.

Listening and *questioning* properly is the way to win the interview. For the first few minutes of the interview, you're *observing* and *determining* how to proceed. You've been given *impossible* questions and have delivered *inspirational* answers.

Now you must ask questions ... *carefully*.

In the recruiter's rulebook **Closing on Objections**, Paul Hawkinson (1984) wrote:

Constant questioning can be grating, and if overused, can work against you.

No one wants to feel that they are on the receiving end of the prosecutor's interrogation and questions must be used sparingly to be really effective.

But they are necessary because selling is the art of asking the right questions to get to the minor yes's that allow you lead . . . to the major decision and major yes.

The final placement is nothing more than the sum total of all your *yes's* throughout the process.

Your job then, is to nurse the process along.

That advice is written for Recruiters in their task of interviewing job applicants.

When you ask questions of the Interviewer, for those brief moments, you are the Interviewer and you don't want to put them on the defence.

But before we get into some techniques for making the sale i.e. landing the job, let's take a look at some questions that you might ask your Interviewer.

They are meant to help you prepare for the interview.

Some questions *may or may not* be appropriate for your interviewing situation. While asking questions of your interviewer may help you look eager and enthusiastic, it may be a tactic to use with caution.

Your Interviewer has come prepared to ask *you* questions. They may not be prepared to respond to *your* questions. The last thing you want to do is to *intimidate* your Interviewer.

If you do ask your Interviewer questions, this is where your notebook might come in handy in recording your Interviewer's response.

Let's look at some questions:

Note: * Indicates that some background information or industry advice has been provided for you to consider.

1. Why is this position open?

2. How often has it been filled in the past five years? What were the main reasons?

3. What would you like done differently by the next person who fills this position?

4. What are some of the objectives you would like to see accomplished in this job?

5. What is most pressing? What would you like to have done in the next 3 months?

6. What would you want the person in this position to accomplish the first 30 days on the job?

* [Respond with excitement about working on the type of projects/assignments mentioned.]

7. What qualities are you seeking in top candidates for this position?

* [If the Interviewer lists a quality/strength you have, but have not covered during your interview, respond by letting the employer know you have that skill.

If the Interviewer mentions something that matched your discussion, you can respond that you are pleased to hear they are seeking someone with your skills and abilities.]

8. What are some of the long-term objectives you would like to see completed?

9. What are some of the more difficult problems one would have to face in this position?

10. What type of support does this position receive in terms of people, finances, etc.?

11. What freedom would I have in determining my own work objectives, deadlines, and methods of measurement?

12. What advancement opportunities are available for the person who is successful in this position, and within what time frame?

13. In what ways has this organization been most successful in terms of products and services over the years?

14. What significant changes do you foresee in the near future?

15. How is one evaluated in this position?

16. What accounts for success within the company?

17. Are you *ready* and *able* to hire now?

18. How long will it take to make a hiring decision?

19. What is the next step in the hiring process?

* [If the Interviewer's answer is vague, ask if you can follow up in a week. This question and response reinforces the fact you are very interested in the job.]

IN THE NEXT CHAPTER, WE LOOK AT USING A TECHNIQUE FROM THE SALES field to move your interview along. Hopefully, to the point that you get offered the job.

2. USING "TIE DOWN" TECHNIQUES TO MOVE THE INTERVIEW ALONG

In this chapter, we look at using "Tie Down" Techniques to Move the Interview Along, in your favour.

Moving the process along is done through the use of '**tie down**' phrases in questions designed to elicit an *affirmative* response.

The method comes from the sales field. You have likely had it used on *you* many times and haven't been aware of it. The idea is that the sales person, in this case it's *you* trying to sell *yourself* as the best candidate for the job, tries to get the other person to answer *'yes'* to a series of small questions.

Once the person has answered 'yes' to the questions, it becomes very difficult for them to say 'no' to the big question.

TWO CHALLENGES ARISE WHEN USING THIS TECHNIQUE.

Firstly, you need to get used to using it. I would suggest doing some role playing with a partner and try to sell them something. Doesn't matter what it is, it could be a pretend product, something you have made up.

The idea is to try to take the other person on a journey to the point where they have no choice but to buy your product or service.

The *second* challenge is that you need to use this technique in a way that the person isn't aware that a technique is being used on them.

Most of us don't like to be sold to. We like to be helped making a purchasing decision though.

We can use the same sales technique in moving our job interview along to the point where we will be offered the job.

Here are the most common techniques. I'm just going to comment on the ones that are likely usable in your job interview.

Aren't I/you/we/they?

Can't I/he/she/you/we/they/it?

Doesn't he/she/it?

Don't I/you/we/they?

Don't you agree?

Hasn't she/he/ it?

Haven't I/you/we/they?

Isn't he/she/it?

Isn't that right?

Shouldn't I/he/she/you/we/they/it?

Wasn't I /he/she/it?

Weren't you/we/they?

Won't I/he/she/you/we/they/ it?

Wouldn't I,/he/she/you/we/they/it?

. . .

There are many kinds of tie downs.

Now we are going to look at *four* of them that have value in moving *forward* in a job interview.

You should vary your dialogue when using them so you don't appear obvious or overbearing.

With each agreement, you obtain from the Interviewer, you have scored one more "minor yes" leading up to that "major yes" offer.

The Standard Tie Down: These are used at the *end* of a question:

"My qualifications appear to fit the position you have open, ***don't they***?"

"Diversified Enterprises really has a lot to offer someone with my experience, ***doesn't it?***"

"It looks like we'll be able to eliminate the problem, ***don't you agree?***"

The Inverted Tie Down: These are used at the *beginning* of a question:

"***Isn't it*** an excellent position for someone with my background?"

"***Don't you*** think we'll be working together well?"

The Internal Tie Down: These are used in the *middle* of a compound sentence:

"Now that we have had the opportunity to meet, ***wouldn't it*** be great to work together?"

The Tag-on Tie Down: The final kind of tie down is used *after* a statement of fact. A slight pause, then emphasis on the tie down, improves it effect:

"My experience will benefit Diversified Enterprises, ***won't it?***"

"You've really spent a lot of time and money to get the right person, ***haven't you?***"

"This problem can be corrected easily, ***can't it?***"

THE BEST WAY TO LEARN TIE DOWN QUESTIONING TECHNIQUES IS THE same way you rehearse your script for the interview.

You write down all the tie down lines you can use during the interview, then read them into a voice recorder and play them back once or twice a day, every day, to implant them into your subconscious.

They'll pop out automatically when you need them.

~

IN THE NEXT SECTION, SECTION VIII WE LOOK AT MAKING THE FOLLOW-up phone call after your interview.

SECTION VIII

The Follow-up Phone Call

1. THE FOLLOW-UP PHONE CALL

Assuming you have made it to the interview stage, here is a strategy to consider after your interview.

The follow-up telephone call is one of the most *important devices* in job searching --- and also one of the *most unused.*

Many job searchers *don't* feel confident enough about themselves to make this important phone call.

As with your initial follow-up response, the keys to success when you telephone your target are *timing* and *technique*. That means knowing:

- When to call
- Whom to call
- And What to say

Your ongoing purpose of this *follow-up* phone call is to maintain the prospect's impression of you as:

- Enthusiastic
- Confident
- Energetic

- Dependable
- Loyal
- Honest
- Proud of your work
- Concerned with service

The fact that you're taking the *trouble* to make this follow-up call, by itself, *demonstrates* these qualities.

Or at least it should!

Let's look at timing the Telephone Follow-up.

Don't Wait Too Long!

The best advice to heed is the "fiddle theory," introduced by Robert Singer in Winning Through Intimidation:

The longer a person *fiddles* around with something, the greater the odds that the result will be negative . . .

In the case of *Nero*, Rome burned; in the case of a *sale*, the longer it takes to get to a point of closing, the greater the odds it will *never* close.

As a *general* rule, you should always assume that time is always against you when you try to make a deal --- *any* kind of deal.

There's an old saying about "striking while the iron's hot."

If you haven't received a response to your follow-up letter within a *week* after the interview, call, but ... never on a Monday.

Mondays are full of staff meetings, unexpected crises, and weekend wounds. Don't call, write, or interview on a Monday if you can help it.

Statistically, the best time to call is Tuesday through Friday, from 9.00 am to 11.00 am.

. . .

Targeting the Telephone Follow-up

You *already* know who should receive your call.

You spent a long time talking with him or her during the first interview.

Despite these interview tips, you may still feel in a one-down position with your Interviewer. Don't!

Initiating the call automatically gives you the upper hand.

You're *prepared* and can *guide* the conversation to the outcome you want.

In the next section, Section IX we explore working with Staffing/Temp Agencies and Recruiters.

SECTION IX

Working with Staffing Agencies & Recruiters

1. WORKING WITH STAFFING AGENCIES & RECRUITERS

It's our *current* reality that many businesses are using staffing agencies or recruiters to fill their vacant job positions.

According to the American Staffing Association's website, more than *90% of companies* in the USA use staffing firms, and *40% of employees* looking for their first job or who are re-entering the job market have done so by working with a staffing company.

Staffing can be a *bridge* to permanent employment and the *potential* for securing a *permanent* position is a major reason people seek temporary work.

According to a 2014 American Staffing Association survey of staffing employees, half (49%) of those surveyed chose *temporary* or *contract* work as a way to obtain a permanent job.

One third (35%) were offered a permanent job by a client where they worked on an assignment, and two-thirds (66%) accepted the offers of permanent employment.

(Source: American Staffing Association, 2014 Staffing Employee Survey)

Let's start off by taking a close look at how Employment Agencies work and how you can leverage temporary work into a permanent position.

Employment Agencies are also called Staffing Agencies or Temp Agencies

Both public and private employment agencies help place workers.

In the United States, one of the major public employment agencies is the U.S. Department of Labor Employment and Training Administration.

This agency provides job-seeking services and tools for workers through online resources and a network of offices around the country. It promotes public and private sector jobs by linking to national and state job banks.

Private employment agencies *also* help place workers, particularly in the private sector.

These employment agencies tend to specialize in one of three fields:

- personnel placement services
- staffing services, also known as temporary help services
- executive search firms

The staffing agency earns money by charging clients for the amount of work the employee does.

Other types of employment agencies, such as *consultants* or *recruiters*, are for businesses looking to hire *permanent* help.

When a business needs a specific person for a job, it'll contract with a personnel placement services firm, also called a *recruiter*.

The recruiter handles the search process and matches up an employee with the job in question, lining up potential candidates who interview with the company.

For senior-level management positions, a company may choose to hire an executive search firm, also known as a *head-hunter*.

An executive search firm works under a retainer agreement from the hiring company and uses a set code of standards to identify and place workers in these highly visible positions.

When a company only needs a vacation fill-in or someone to work for a few months, it uses a staffing agency.

Staffing agencies provide skilled employees to work on a temporary or contract basis.

Some employers also use staffing agencies as recruiters in positions known as "temp to perm," meaning the position is temporary, but it could lead to a permanent position if the worker and company are a good fit.

For job seekers, an employment agency can be the ticket to getting that full-time job. Recruiters can open doors to positions that may not be easy to find on your own.

Staffing companies allow you to try out different companies and industries, and they're also great for those looking for short-term or part-time work.

Another bonus of using an employment agency is access to training. Many employment agencies offer free training in a variety of skill-building tools, such as software programs and computer skills.

Those who take advantage of these skills can build up their resumes, making them more marketable for the employment agency. Many job hunters consider employment agencies an invaluable resource.

While an agency *can't* always guarantee employment, it *can* provide you with opportunities to land a job that's right for you.

When using an employment agency, you'll have to do *one or more* the following steps:

- find and register with one or more agencies
- fill out an application
- provide a resume
- take qualifying tests
- interview
- go through training, if necessary

Look for a staffing agency that will suit your needs and skills. If you don't have a legal background, it's no good going to an agency that specializes in the legal field.

Ask around for recommendations, and do a little digging online to see if the agency is reliable and has a good reputation. You may want to sign up with more than one agency to increase your chances of being placed.

Although agencies have access to a wide variety of assignments, it may take a *while* to find a placement that *matches* your qualifications.

A staffing agency, particularly one specializing in temporary placement services, will have you fill out an application.

The *agency* will be the ones hiring you, so the company will want your resume on file, and it'll want to test your abilities in certain job skills, such as software programs.

When a temporary position is a match for you, the agency will call you to tell you about the position and arrange the assignment.

If you don't hear from an agency right away, there may not be any opportunities at the moment, but check in *weekly* to show your continued interest in a placement.

Once you're placed, you'll need to keep a record of your time on the job, and the agency will pay you directly. Once your assignment is over, you'll go back into the agency's pool to be considered for future assignments.

Private employment agencies may charge fees for their services.

Usually, the hiring company pays the agency, but sometimes job seekers pay recruiters to find opportunities for them.

If you are faced with having to pay an employment agency for their services, make sure that you have a clear understanding of what you will be getting for your money. If you're a job seeker who's paying for employment services, use a certified recruiter who will keep your best interests in mind.

A reliable agency can't guarantee that you get a job, but it'll work to help you find the position that's best for you. If you find yourself in the lucky position of being the best candidate for the job, you'll be hired by the staffing agency, not the employer (the only exception to this is a "direct hire" position.

Your paycheck and your benefits (if offered) will be issued from the staffing agency, but the length of your employment is determined by the employer.

In the next chapter, we look at what kinds of jobs staffing agencies have to offer you.

2. WHAT KINDS OF JOBS DO STAFFING AGENCIES OFFER?

As it turns out, not all staffing agency jobs are the same.

Clients (your future employer) have different needs depending on the positions they're trying to fill, so it's important to know exactly what type of job you'll have when you get your assignment.

These are the three major ***types*** of jobs offered by staffing agencies:

Temporary: With a temporary job, you will typically know the start and end date of your assignment up front.

These will sometimes change in the middle of a job (usually longer rather than shorter), but if you're looking for a steady routine, this probably isn't the kind of job for you.

Temporary-to-permanent (temp-to-perm): Lots of people take staffing agency jobs hoping they'll be temp-to-perm or temp-to-hire.

Temp-to-perm jobs are a way for an employer to *gauge* your ability to work for the company on a regular full-time basis.

Permanent (direct hire): For permanent positions, the staffing agency acts as a recruiter by screening and hiring candidates for regular positions. Employees are then hired directly by the employer.

Each temp agency has their own guidelines and different contracts with companies; therefore, the following information could vary from one agency to another.

In the next segment, we dig deeper into what's involved when you work with an employment agency.

What should I expect in my interview or visit to an Employment agency?

When you walk into a temp agency, a staffing specialist will likely greet you and have you fill out an application/information sheet that helps to highlight your strengths.

You should bring your resume if you have one. If you don't have a resume, some agencies will help you to create one.

References for the type of work you are seeking and a background check are also generally required by the agency.

The Employment agency will interview you in person. Your interview at the temp agency is similar to an interview you would have when you apply directly to a company looking for a new employee.

The staff member will ask you questions about your employment history, strengths and about circumstances under which you left previous jobs. Just be honest and have answers prepared for the potential questions.

Many of the interviews are done over Skype as well.

Don't stress over the interviews here. It is easier to do well in these than regular interviews because most staffing companies always want to increase their pool of employees to choose from and want to help you improve your chances of getting a job through them.

Plus, it is less commitment and is less expensive for them to hire and let go of you than it is for a regular company. Additionally, you may be asked to take tests to assess your skill level for the type of work you perform.

For example, if one of your skills is typing, you will be given an exam to see how many words per minute you type as well as the accuracy.

Another example that is very common is a Microsoft Office skills test, such as Word or Excel. Other tests may be required based on your specialty or industry.

The temp agency uses the results of your tests to match you with jobs they have from different companies.

You will most likely want to know what kind of a work schedule you will get and the employment agency will also want to know what your availability is.

Be prepared to answer these common questions about what kind of schedule you would like:

- Are you available on weekends?
- Do you want to work strictly days, nights or are you available anytime?
- Is there a particular geographical area where you would prefer to work?

Temp schedules are unpredictable until you are on a project or job with a company.

They may call you at any moment and on short notice to go for an interview at one of the companies they work with.

What to Expect When You Sign Up with a Temp Agency

Job hunters often feel they must embellish their skills to land a job, but when you sign up to work with a temp agency, exaggerating your skills may work against you.

You could end up in the wrong position.

So, during your first meeting at a temp agency, be honest!

What if you feel you've been honest with your temp agency representative, but the assignment you're sent on still isn't a good fit? The agency should take you off the job but not leave you hanging.

They should also provide you feedback from the employer. It's important to step back and accept such a critique of your work habits, especially after a job does not work out.

View it as free advice that you can use to make yourself a better full-time employee down the road. Being armed with such information helps prep you not only for your next assignment but also for your overall career goals.

In the next segment, we discuss Employment Agency contracts.

Contracts:

When you decide to work or a temp agency, you will almost always be asked to sign a contract.

This contract basically states that you are affiliated with the temp agency and have certain restrictions with the companies that they introduce you to.

When they send you on a job, you cannot accept any other temporary or permanent position with the company without going through the temp agency.

Should the company want to hire you permanently, they will pay the temp agency a certain amount to release you from your contract.

There will likely be a clause in your contract addressing this possibility.

As in any contract, make sure you really understand what you are signing.

Going into great detail on what you should expect in a contract is beyond the scope of this program.

The information I'm providing you here should not be considered as legal advice.

You can expect that the contract has been written favouring the employment agency.

As soon as you sign the contract, you are liable to follow its terms.

Here are some categories of terms that you can expect to see in an Employee/Temp Agency's employment contract: (Remember ... this is a contract between you and the Employment Agency, not the work-site employer that you will temporarily be working.)

1. **Commencement Date and Term** – This indicates the day that you will start work and how long you will be working for the agency.
2. **Job Title and Description** – Every job should have a title and a description of the duties involved.
3. The Employee agrees to abide by the Employer's rules, regulations, policies and practices, including those concerning work schedules, vacation and sick leave, as they may from time to time be adopted or modified. (In working with an Employment Agency, they are your Employer, not the worksite. You may or may not have benefits included. Don't assume that you will.)
4. **Employee Compensation** – The contract should define what rate of pay you will be receiving and how often you will be paid. If you work different jobs for the same Employment Agency, there may be different rates of pay involved.
5. **Place of Work** – The contract should outline where you will be performing the agreed upon work.

6. **Time of Work** - The contract should outline your normal hours of work, including how many and what length of breaks.
7. **There may be a Conflict of Interest Clause:** This clause would outline activities that you would not be able to undertake if they were to cause a conflict with the business activities of the Employer.

How does the pay work?

The temp agency is responsible for paying the workers they send to a company.

They charge the company a set amount per hour from which they take a percentage. The temp agency is also responsible for collecting taxes from the temporary worker's pay.

All of this is specified in the contract that the company has with the temp agency.

For example, if a temp worker is paid $15 per hour, the company for which they are working may actually be paying $25 per hour for their services. The temp agency keeps the extra $10 per hour of the pay. The markup is typically 50% to 100%, and is 66% in this example.

Use all temporary jobs to expand your network

Now that you know how a temp agency works, you should feel more confident about updating your resume, putting on a professional outfit and visiting several temp agencies in your community.

Don't forget, while working jobs through a temp agency, expand your network and meet as many people as you can in your industry.

~

WE'VE BEEN TALKING ABOUT EMPLOYMENT AGENCIES.

In the next chapter, we look at how Job Recruiters work.

3. WORKING WITH JOB RECRUITERS

Let's move on to some things you should know about Job Recruiters.

Many job seekers are confused about how hiring works, and specifically, about how to work with recruiters. Recruitment agencies are outside firms who go and find candidates for employers.

Do not confuse *recruitment* agencies with *employment* agencies. The main difference lies in who ends up being your employer. If you get a job through a recruitment agency, you become an employee of the employer.

If you get a job through an employment agency, you become an employee of the employment agency.

There are employment agencies out there who provide IT support people to firms, but professional engineering roles are normally found through recruitment agencies.

Should you use a recruitment agency at all?

If you know which employers you want to work for, and if they accept direct applications, then there's no reason to apply through a recruitment agency.

There's no benefit in doing so and with no middle-man for all communication to pass through, you might find that you prefer always dealing with the employer directly.

The better recruiting agencies can be a great help in getting hired, especially later in your career when you're chasing more senior jobs.

Recruiter's Roles:

It is important to understand Recruiter's roles and how the process works, in order to be successful.

Let's look at some of those roles.

1. Recruiters are not career counsellors.

Don't expect a recruiter to look at your resume and immediately understand where you would fit into their organization or to suggest which career path you should choose. They don't know you well enough, and they aren't mind readers.

It is your job to know what you want to do and to tell the recruiter where you fit into an organization — which jobs you want and, hopefully, which part of the organization.

2. Recruiters are not for hire by job seekers.

They work for the employer who pays them.

Many will go out of their way to help you, if they can, but don't expect them to guide you in your job search.

3. There are many different kinds of recruiters, but they all fall into one of two major categories:

Internal recruiters (also known as "in-house"). They are employees of the employer they represent, paid a salary by that employer.

External recruiters (also known as "agencies," "headhunters," "search consultants," or "sourcers" depending on how they work and how they are paid).

They are employees of recruiting or "staffing" firms or agencies usually helping many different employers find employees.

External recruiters may specialize in a location, a profession, an industry, a job level, a search technology/method, or a combination.

Some firms focus on helping employers find employees for temporary assignments, often called "temping agencies" or "contracting agencies" which may specialize in a location, profession, etc.

We've already talked about this type earlier in this section.

4. Recruiters are seldom the decision-maker, determining whether or not you get a job offer.

They often have input into the decision, depending on the organization and they are often the person who delivers the good or bad news to the job seeker.

But, someone else, often a committee in very large organizations or the hiring manager, makes the hiring decision.

5. Recruiters are seldom in control of the hiring process.

Their job is to find good job candidates, and they try to keep the process flowing smoothly.

However, because the hiring process usually involves many different people and functions, particularly in large or widely distributed organizations, the process is seldom as smooth as anyone wants it to be.

How Should You Work with Internal Recruiters?

Very carefully.

They are not "on your side" in this process. No matter how friendly, they are not your friend (yet).

Always present your "best" self to them. Do not confide in them, or ask them to do you any favours. Be professional and business-like in all your communications with them.

Wear your interview outfit if you are invited in for a meeting with them.

Typically, they are your official contact for the process. So, when you have questions or concerns, you are usually advised to contact the recruiter. Be careful not to abuse this contact function because it can have a negative impact on your opportunity with that employer.

Do your best to avoid the "difficult-to-work-with" label, because that will greatly reduce (if not eliminate) your opportunities inside that organization.

How Should You Work with External Recruiters?

The best part about working with an external recruiter is that you both usually have the same goal — getting you placed with the employer.

Again, don't tell them your deepest secrets, but do be honest with them about your interests and experience. If you have gaps or other issues, they may be able to help you strategize a way to present yourself in the best light.

Don't expect them to help you figure out what you want to do, but do expect them to provide you with some insight into what is going on inside the employer's organization - what the "hot" issues are, who are apt to be your allies in the hiring process, and who the real decision makers are.

After you have been in for an interview, they may be your primary source of information on what is going on "behind the curtain" during the often extended hiring process.

Try very hard not to drive them crazy with daily calls, but do stay in touch. If you land a job through an external recruiter, be sure to send them a thank you.

A good relationship with an external recruiter can be an asset to your career for many years.

Connect with them on LinkedIn. Send cards during the holidays.

Refer top performers you know to these external recruiters to strengthen your relationship with them and help them to remember you with positive feelings.

How Do External Recruiters Get Paid?

Recruitment agencies get paid by the employer for every candidate they put forward who successfully gets a job with the employer.

Some agencies get paid on a fixed-fee basis, and some agencies get paid a fee based on your starting salary.

You don't have to pay them at all, and you should never use any recruitment agency who asks you for any payment.

Connect with Recruiters

Most external recruiters and many internal recruiters, are open to Linkedin connection invitations.

Being connected to as many people as possible in Linkedin is an advantage to them because it enables them to do a substantial amount of research in Linkedin without paying the extra fee Linkedin likes to collect from recruiters.

How to Find a Job with a Recruiter – 2018 Edition

Finding a job can be challenging at the best of times. Leveraging a recruiter to help find a job can save you time and grief.

Using a qualified recruiting agency will offer some advantages that you may not be able to obtain on your own. With a recruiter, you gain a skilled and experienced representative that will assist you in the highly competitive search for jobs.

A recruiter can act as your liaison to HR managers and has access to resources and industry information that they can share with you to support your job hunt.

In 2018, the question may very well be why wouldn't you use a recruiter to find a job?

I suspect that statement may have come from a Recruiter ...

There are a number of benefits in using a recruiter in your next job search.

Here's a few important things to look for in using a recruiter. A recruiting agency can help you find a job by assisting you with the following:

Coaching

Recruiters can help coach you on the finer points of assembling your job-search materials. From resume and cover letter writing to compilation of asset statements, a recruiter can help you polish aspects of your job search.

When selecting a recruiter, check to see if they offer the ability to help with your resume and other job search materials.

Don't assume that they will. Some will ... some won't.

Labour / Market Information

A well-organized recruiter will be able to provide you with relevant and up-to-date information specific to the industry in which you are searching for a job.

Information may include salary trends, insight into employment trends, certifications requirements or other prerequisites that may be required for the position being applied for.

Knowledge is power ... right?

The more information you have about the job, the employer, job requirements and expectations, the better your chances of securing employment.

Marketing your Skillset

Recruiters can help you identify any crucial gaps in your skills.

When preparing your resume and cover letter they can help you add highly marketable capabilities and skills to your resume. As a result, you can better market yourself which can lead to increased compensation offers.

Reference Advocate

As recruiters often act as a liaison with the hiring manager, building a strong relationship with a recruiter can turn them into one of your greatest advocates which in turn can prove beneficial when the recruiter discusses your unique talents with hiring managers.

Working with a recruitment agency will assist you in finding a job by helping you:

- Be more prepared for the interview process
- Gain industry knowledge and insight that can give you a competitive edge in your job search
- Maintain confidence as they help build your arsenal of job search material including resumes, accomplishment statements and cover letters
- Understand/Communicate why you are the best candidate for the position

LEVERAGE AN EMPLOYMENT AGENCY TO FIND THE TEMPORARY, PART-time, or full-time job that you've been looking for.

In the next section, Section X we explore some tips from the pros.

SECTION X

Job Searching Tips from the Pros

1. JOB SEARCHING TIPS FROM THE PROS

In this chapter, we look at a compilation of tips related to different aspects of the job searching process provided by industry professionals.

Tips from the Pros:

"What people tend to fumble with sometimes is not understanding, at first, the point of the questions,"

Find someone who will do mock interviews with you. Think about what the questions are really asking.

For example, an interviewer who asks about a situation involving conflict with a client or colleague doesn't want to hear about the time you got *really* mad.

Conflict can just be a different way of doing things, a different work style, they want an example where you took initiative to address the conflict.

~

Suggest practicing the skill of interjecting, in case you find yourself with a talkative interviewer. "You can't let them do all the talking or they won't know anything about you."

Look for the small moments when you can wedge in – for example, places to say, "Great point, and ..." or, "I'd love to add to that ..." Also practice using nonverbal signals, such as leaning forward or raising a finger.

Strike a 'Power Pose': Body language theory suggests striking a "power pose" – i.e., hands on hips like Wonder Woman – can have a confidence-boosting effect. Find a private spot to power pose for two minutes right before the interview.

During the Interview, Envision Your Best Future.

If you're still feeling awkward about promoting yourself, think in terms of how advancing your career will help the organization.

Talk about contributing your skills and experience to benefit the organization [and] enrich and inspire the team, that takes it away from me, me, me.

Look Up - Don't forget to pay attention to your nonverbal behaviour. Eye contact is high on the list of importance in a job interview.

If eye contact is uncomfortable for you, look at the other person's eyebrows, nose, or ears.

OFFER CLARITY - IF YOU ARE AN INTROVERT, YOU MAY HAVE A TENDENCY to be succinct, which can backfire in an interview. If you're unsure whether your brief response fully answered a question, offer to add more information. If the interviewer doesn't encourage you to continue, you have permission to stop.

BUY SOME TIME - IF YOU NEED A MINUTE TO THINK ABOUT A QUESTION, buy yourself a bit of time by paraphrasing the question. Don't be embarrassed to return to an earlier topic you feel you could have addressed better.

"Just say something like, 'I had another thought about that question.'

SUMMARIZE - AT THE END OF THE INTERVIEW, TAKE A MOMENT TO recap.

Try to end strongly: "I want to reiterate why I'm interested in the position and why I'm qualified ..."

MULTIPLE FONTS - FOR THE MOST PART, RECRUITERS AREN'T GOING TO read your whole resume.

They'll look at your title, company, and dates of employment for each job, and then move on. The human eye is a funny thing. If you have several different fonts on the page, it may mess with the reader's comprehension.

They'll have to reread certain sections of the resume just to make sure they understand – if you're lucky, that is. If you aren't lucky, they will just move on to the next candidate.

'REFERENCES GIVEN UPON REQUEST' - WE KNOW THEY ARE. WE WILL ask you for references if we decide to give you an offer. This is premature in the relationship. All you've done so far was send a cover letter and resume.

~

DON'T USE FUNNY OR ODD E-MAIL ADDRESSES – OR WORSE, YOUR current company's e-mail address.

~

WHEN WORKING WITH JOB RECRUITERS, TO ENSURE YOU MAKE THE MOST of your time with them, it's best to find out what they want to hear. Knowing what recruiters are looking for in potential candidates can be what helps you succeed over your competitors.

HERE ARE SOME OF THE MOST COMMON THINGS RECRUITERS WANT OUT of their candidates—and how to get there.

What Motivates You in the Workplace?

Recruiters are looking for more than a person to fill a role—they want to recruit a new employee who will exceed in the position and enjoys coming to work every day.

For them, a good way to screen candidates is to know what motivates them in the workplace.

You'll be asked certain questions like why do you want to work here? What attracted you to this position? Where do you see yourself in five years?

Each of these questions is trying to discover the root of what motivates you.

If your answer is simply related to getting a paycheque, chances are you'll be passed over for someone who has more passion.

Asking Questions

Asking questions is another really great way to show that you're dedicated to the role.

Recruiters are looking to see you're engaged with them during the interview, and simply nodding along is only going to hurt your chances.

Make your questions count—especially when they pertain to the organization itself.

You can learn a lot from recruiters by asking questions, so make the most of your time with them.

Not only that, asking questions will demonstrate to a recruiter that your critical and quick-thinking skills are sharp, which is often a deciding factor when the time comes down to choose between two great candidates.

If You're a Good Cultural Fit

Many candidates *underestimate* how important it is to be a good cultural fit for an organization.

Having the right skills and experience for the position is important, but ensuring you'll get along with coworkers and match cohesively with the company's internal mission and values can be just as important.

While being authentic is key during your meeting with the recruiter, there are a few things you can do to help ensure you come across as a great cultural fit.

First, appearance can be a good indicator—dressing in a way that suits the office culture can leave an ideal first impression.

You'll also want to be honest with yourself—if your meeting with the recruiter indicates the position isn't what you want after all, don't move forward with it.

It's possible the recruiter will have an even better opening for you, and your honesty can go along way in telling a recruiter what he needs to hear about you as a candidate.

Record some notes

As soon as you get out of the meeting, write down everything you can remember.

This will help you remember all the details, and details can be very useful, especially when you want to write a detailed, thoughtful follow-up email. [or phone call as we discussed in a previous section]

Also, once you've left the interview, jot down the names of the people you met with, their job titles, what you talked about, and anything else that seemed significant. Make note of any questions you still have.

Reflect

Whether you get this job or not, you should be able to learn something from this interview. The best way to do that is to be sure to take some time to reflect on the interview.

How do you rate your own performance? Was there something you feel you can improve on?

Discuss it with someone you trust. Or do a little writing about what went well and what could've gone better.

The goal here isn't to make yourself feel bad; it's to identify weak spots in your interviewing and communication skills so that you can do better next time.

Was there a question that tripped you up? Had a hard time describing your experience?

Do some research into common interview questions and practice, practice, practice!

This process will also help you understand if the company position is really right for you.

Now is the time to be honest with yourself.

If you can, ask for feedback

There may be a lot of good that can come from this process, even if you don't get the job.

Occasionally, when you're turned down for a position, you'll be notified by phone or email.

If that happens to you, seize the opportunity. Thank them for taking them time to contact you, and then ask for more information about why you weren't hired.

Tell them that you'd like to learn from this process and that any feedback would be very much appreciated. Not only will you reiterate your professionalism, you'll likely learn something that will help you the next time around.

OUR NEXT SECTION, SECTION XI, IS FOCUSING ON PERSONAL MARKETING and self-promotion by job-searchers.

SECTION XI

Introduction to Personal Marketing & Promotion

1. PERSONAL MARKETING & PROMOTION

In this section, we explore the concept of personal marketing and promotion and how it can improve your job searching success.

A few years back when I was researching my e-book **Power Networking for Shy People: Tips & Techniques for Moving from Shy to Sly,** I discovered a book by William Bridges ... **Creating You & Company: Learn to think like the CEO of your own company.**

Bridges encourages you to market yourself as if you are the company. He takes the corporate idea of branding and challenges us to apply it to ourselves.

I agree and say ... "Blow your own horn!"

"If you don't, who will?"

Reading the book helped provide clarity and peace of mind for me.

Bridge's book helped me to redefine myself in a new way. "Hello, I'm Rae Stonehouse. I am a nurse entrepreneur and a believer in the law of attraction! I am open to the opportunities and abundance that the universe has to offer."

I'll leave it as that at for your understanding of who I am.

We've looked at different elements of personal branding in other sections and here we are going to look at it in some more detail.

This Section is lifted from another course I have under development entitled **Blow Your Own Horn: Marketing & Promotional Strategies for Business Professionals.**

I've adapted the content to add value to your job searching success as it may be an area that you haven't given a lot of thought to or that causes you some difficulties.

~

IN THE NEXT CHAPTER, WE LOOK AT BRANDING.

2. BRANDING OVERVIEW

Let's start off by determining what a ***brand*** is.

From Wikipedia ...

A **brand** is a name, term, design, symbol, or other feature that distinguishes one seller's product from those of others.

Brands are used in business, marketing and advertising. A brand is any name, design, style, words or symbols used singularly or in combination that distinguish one product from another in the eyes of the customer.

Branding is a set of marketing and communication methods that help to distinguish a company from competitors and create a lasting impression in the minds of customers.

The key components that form a brand's toolbox include a brand's identity, brand communication (such as by logos and trademarks), brand awareness, brand loyalty and various brand management strategies.

We are all familiar with commercial branding and are likely bombarded with it everyday. Coca Cola, Pepsi Cola and Nike readily come to mind.

These are well established brands.

In the next segment, we are going to expand upon the concept of personal branding.

Personal Branding Defined

According to Wikipedia, ***personal branding*** is the practice of people marketing themselves and their careers as ***brands***.

Let's expand upon the concept of Personal Branding.

While previous self-help management techniques were about self-improvement, the personal-branding concept suggests instead that success comes from *self-packaging*.

The term is thought to have been first used and discussed in a 1997 article by Tom Peters.

Personal branding is essentially the ongoing process of establishing a prescribed image or impression in the mind of others about an individual, group, or organization.

Personal branding often involves the application of one's name to various products.

Athletes and celebrities come to mind.

If that is your situation, well good for you!

I would expect that you have staff to look after you. For the rest of us mere mortals, let's drill down a little.

In the next chapter, we explore personal branding, what it really means, why we should do it and what often *prevents* us from doing it.

3. SELF-PROMOTION

So why don't we self-promote?

There are likely numerous reasons that many of us don't like to talk about ourselves to others.

Many of us have likely been taught at a young age from our mothers that it is wrong to promote yourself.

"It is bragging and nobody likes braggarts!"

That may be a generalization and it really isn't fair to pick on mothers, considering all the good they do for us.

However, while many people likely don't like braggarts, it doesn't necessarily follow that talking about yourself in a favourable light ... is bragging.

I'm fond of a quote from Walt Whitman about personal branding. He was an American Cowboy poet, essayist and journalist, way back in the mid to later 1800s.

He probably didn't relate it any way to personal branding but here goes...

"If you done it ... it ain't bragging!"

I think Walt hit the proverbial nail on the head. If you have done something and you talk about it, then it isn't bragging.

That sounds like ***self-promotion*** to me.

Can you think of any other reasons that we don't self-promote?

It could be a simple matter of we really don't know how to promote ourselves.

I'm hoping this chapter helps resolve the problem if you identify with that reason.

ANOTHER SIMPLE REASON MAY BE THAT WE DON'T HAVE *TIME* TO SELF-promote.

Through this program I have been providing strategies that you will be able to follow and start yourself off well with your self-promoting.

As your skill in self-promotion increases and your self-confidence as well, you should find it easy to self-promote.

THEN THERE IS A SIMPLE REASON THAT MOST OF US HAVE LIKELY experienced at one time or another.

It can be embarrassing at first when you create promotional copy, featuring yourself in a good light.

But when you think about it, that's exactly what you had to do when you created your resume.

In earlier chapters, we focused on on-line reputation management.

One of the features of social media platforms is that they often require you to create a Bio or a Profile as a term of your membership.

While these can be a great opportunity for self-promotion, the first few times can be challenging.

Do you write your promotional copy in the first person as "I did this, this and this ..."

Or do you write it in the 3rd person, "Rae Stonehouse, renowned best-selling author is known for ..."

Okay, so I'm not a best-selling author yet, but I have a head start on promoting it.

Before we move on to the next segment, if you haven't done it recently, Google your name and see what comes up.

It is always a good idea to research yourself, just in case you need to do some damage control.

So ... how do we self-promote?

We discussed maximizing our digital footprint, earlier in the book.

Let's take it from there.

While you are in job searching mode, your on-line promotional copy, including your Linkedin profile, your resume and any other social media platform you are on should all resonate and promote you as a person to hire, or at the very least, to interview.

What you do with your digital footprint after you get your dream job is up to you.

Since we haven't defined the word 'copy' yet, it might be an idea to do so now. It is any text that you write about yourself that is promotional in nature, rather than factual.

My use of the word *factual* here might be a little confusing. When you are creating your resume, you certainly want to be factual.

You need to highlight your experience and accomplishments. Highlighting, in this sense, would mean adding quantifiers as we discussed a few lessons back.

These are the **CAR or SAR** statements.

Remember, this is where you're sharing a challenge/situation/problem, the action you took to address it, and what the result was.

This is quantifiable self-promotion.

If you did it, it ain't bragging.

Back in Section One: Part Three we explored developing your network web.

A couple self-promotional ideas were introduced there.

One of them being that as a job searcher, you should be out there networking, developing connections. And if you are networking, you need to have an elevator pitch. Several versions actually.

These are perfect opportunities to promote yourself.

One version you would use for 1 to 1 interactions. This is where you are meeting someone for the first time. Your content would tend to be more personal. Frame it from the perspective of how you can help someone else, rather than what you need.

Another version of your elevator pitch is used when you introduce yourself to larger groups of people.

Somewhere in your elevator pitch, you will need to mention that you are in job search mode and in what specific field. It is not the time to ask for a job though.

We talked back in Section One: Part Three - Chapter 13 about developing your USP, your Universal Selling Point.

You can fit this into your elevator pitch, as a way to help people remember you.

. . .

AND DON'T FORGET TO HAVE YOUR BUSINESS CARD TO PASS ON TO YOUR new connection.

One of the most inexpensive forms of self-promotion is the business card.

As a job searcher, having a business card to be able to exchange with a potential connection, is a necessity.

ALSO, BACK IN AN EARLIER CHAPTER, IT WAS SUGGESTED THAT AFTER every networking session you follow up with people that you met by researching them on Linkedin and sending them an invitation to join your network.

You should have their contact info from when you exchanged business cards.

You don't have any control if they accept your invitation or not, but it does provide another opportunity to reinforce your name in their minds.

Final Thoughts on Self-Promotion

SELF-PROMOTION IS PROBABLY AS MUCH A MIND-SET AS IT IS A SET OF strategies.

You have to believe in yourself. You have to believe that you are just as good as anybody else. And you have to believe that you are worthy of success. If any of these self-beliefs are challenging for you, I would suggest that you revisit Section One that covered envisioning your success.

It can be helpful to go through the self-affirmations and envisioning your success at every step of the job searching process.

While I'm a firm believer in self-promotion, I balance it with not taking myself too seriously.

While I'm not currently looking for a job, I am looking for business opportunities. So, I can be a little riskier with my digital footprint.

I've tried to be consistent with the professional brand that I have across all of my digital presence.

If you are interested, check out my personal website at raestonehouse.com. It starts off with 'Welcome to the Wonderful World of Rae Stonehouse! 50 Shades of Rae, if you will!'

The *promotional copy* goes on to say 'Over the years of entrepreneurial pursuits I have learned the value of self-promotion.

While I have learned that you can't control what anybody else writes about you, yes Trolls are still among us, you can make it easy for someone who really wants to learn more about you.

This website is designed to provide you with more than you probably ever wanted to know about me ... and some!

I also believe that I am a creator of valuable content that should be shared. As a graduate of the School of Hard Knocks my passion is in creating self-help articles in the category of "Tips & Techniques to ... "

You will find an ever-increasing collection of articles that will be of value to you.'

In some ways, it is very much a scrapbook of interests and issues important to me.

I don't believe that I have mentioned it yet in this program, but a great way to self-promote is to create blogs on topics that showcase you as an expert.

Search engines will index your content and cross index it with your name and the keywords you use.

This helps you get discovered online.

If you have website building skills, a personal website such as I have developed can add to your resume and your Linkedin profile.

At the very least, it is worthwhile purchasing a domain name, that is a web address for your own name before somebody else does.

WE ARE DRAWING NEAR THE END OF THIS PROGRAM. IN THE NEXT section, Section XII I offer some final thoughts on effective job searching.

SECTION XII

FINAL COMMENTS & ADDITIONAL RESOURCES

Everything eventually comes to an end and we are pretty well at that point with this program.

Before I wrap up though, there are some things that I want to comment on that don't really fit into any of the other categories that we have talked about throughout the program.

Some ***final*** thoughts if you will.

Research the job before you apply:

I was recently talking to a hiring manager who had just interviewed two prospective nurses for a vacant nursing position.

She had advised me that there was quite a bit of preparation on their side, that is from the Employer's side, in setting up the two interviews.

Two managers had to set time aside for the interviews from their busy schedules and consult with each other about what questions they were going to ask the applicants.

According to the hiring manager, both candidates were hireable but it never happened.

After the interviews, each of the applicants looked at the job work schedule and decided that it wasn't workable. It created conflict with maintaining a family life.

From the hiring manager's perspective, they felt that the applicants should have checked the work schedule in advance. It wouldn't have wasted anybody's time that way.

The same hiring manager suggested that when you are interested in a job and planning on applying for it, whatever the job might be, that you contact the employer and ask for a copy of the job duties & responsibilities.

Some may call these job specs or perhaps job descriptions. Doing so would likely help reinforce your eagerness to take on the position.

It would also help you with the job interviewing process as many job advertisements don't go into much detail as to what the job actually entails.

On-line Applications:

Another factor in the job searching process that I discovered in my research refers to the on-line application process.

As you work your way though some of the forms, you may find that there are questions or categories that you feel you are unable to complete or fill in.

This becomes a problem when your form is submitted and it is processed by an automatic software program. The software will collect data from the application form and insert into a data base organized by categories.

The categories are then referenced when the employer accesses the database.

If you have left key categories blank, your application might go directly to a trash file and you won't even be available for consideration.

So, the short version is to make sure that you complete all areas in an application form.

Where to look for jobs:

You may have noticed that throughout this course I haven't set aside a lesson on where to specifically look for jobs.

The easiest suggestion would be to tell you to check out the different on-line job posting sites.

There are two or three big ones out there that seem to get a lot of traffic and will likely be around for a while.

There may also be smaller on-line job posting sites that may post listings in your community, that may not be posted on the larger, more popular sites.

In the so-called olden days, we used to look in the newspapers for job postings. Now, it is very rare to see job postings in the newspaper.

But you know what, sometimes you do!

I wouldn't pay for a newspaper subscription hoping to find one though. You might have better luck looking in a weekend edition of a paper that has a fairly large circulation.

Many communities have on-line news websites that may post local job postings. My own community has at least four of them that I am familiar with.

Don't forget to check Linkedin for job postings. We've talked about searching for a job on their site.

Earlier in one of the lessons I quoted from an experienced job coach who said that the only really effective way to find a good job is to get out there and network.

The hidden job market is what you need to access and you need to meet people to do so.

Putting Job Searching Strategies to Work

I believe that if you put into practice most, if not all of the strategies offered in this program, you will do well in your job search.

At the very least, I believe that what you have learned, will put you ahead of other applicants who don't understand the process.

Don't forget to use the PDCA tool that we introduced way back in Section One.

This whole program is a learning process that has taken you on a journey. Likely, some of the techniques you have learned in the program haven't worked as well as you hoped.

This is the value of the PDCA tool.

Every time you take action or a step towards finding your job, you need to take a look at what worked, what didn't and make adjustments. Then you have to do it differently with your changes in place.

And perhaps again and again, until you are working in your new job.

Success Team:

Way back in Section One, I talked about envisioning your success and thinking in positive terms.

I didn't go into any detail about what it can be like, not having a job. There can be a lot of pressure on you, including family members who are not supportive.

This of course adds to the pressure that you already have.

In Section Two I introduced you to the idea of having a cheerleader team behind you, that of your references.

I recently answered a question on Quora.com that was addressing the pressures of not having a job and how their family was not only not supportive but they were also insulting to the individual.

It occurred to me the value in creating your own success team.

These are people who could be friends, they could be past co-workers or even managers who support you in your job search. They don't necessarily have to be one of your references, but they may very well be.

Many business professionals join what is called a 'Mastermind' group.

The idea is that they support you in whatever endeavour you are undertaking and they hold you accountable to following through with the steps you say that you are going to make.

And you in turn, support the others in the group and hold them accountable.

The same concept applies to developing your own success team.

Your group would agree to hold you accountable, they would act as a sounding board for you to test out ideas and they would help you practice your interviewing skills. Yes, we are still talking about role playing.

If you had free access to a job coach or could afford one, they would likely provide you with the same support.

In conclusion, I would wish you the best of luck, but I believe in making your own luck.

You have the tools to use to find a job, now you have to put them to work.

I said from the beginning that finding and landing a job was a lot of work.

Now you have some work to do.

Please share your success stories with us.

Goodbye and farewell!

Rae A. Stonehouse

SECTION I

ADDITIONAL RESOURCES

Y*our USP:*

Your **unique selling proposition** (a.k.a. **unique selling point**, universal selling point or **USP**) is a marketing concept used to differentiate yourself from your competitors or others in the market place.

Some good current examples of products with a clear USP are:

- Head & Shoulders: "You get rid of dandruff"

Some unique propositions that were pioneers when they were introduced:

- Domino's Pizza: "You get fresh, hot pizza delivered to your door in 30 minutes or less—or it's free."
- FedEx: "When your package absolutely, positively has to get there overnight"
- M&M's: "Melts in your mouth, not in your hand"
- Metropolitan Life: "Get Met, It Pays"

The term USP has been largely replaced by the concept of a ***Positioning Statement***. Positioning is determining what place a brand (tangible good or service) should occupy in the consumer's mind in comparison to its competition. A position is often described as the meaningful difference between the brand and its competitors.
Source: Wikipedia

I recently was blindsided at a Chamber of Commerce function in my city when we were standing in circle participating in what they call a power networking session. We were asked what makes us or our business unique. I didn't recognize it as a USP question and provided an ineffective response. If I had recognized it for what it was i.e. a USP question I would have responded with "Mr. Emcee is a full-service event organizer. From start to finish ... we do it all!"

Your challenge is to develop a USP that on one hand is short and to the point, yet is clear enough that it captures the essence of your business and will stick in the mind of whoever you are sharing it with. Having it prepared in advance, believing in it and being able to recite it with a moment's notice will go a long way in reducing your anxiety and fear which are all part of shyness.

I would also suggest researching your competitors or others that are in a similar business that are not necessarily your competitors to see if they have chosen a similar USP as you have. I am aware of two business coaches that chose a USP that had only one word that was different. That one word totally changed the context of the USP but it really upset one of the coaches accusing the other of stealing her idea, even though they had been developed independent of each other.

Power Networking Logistics:

1. Research your competitors to learn what their USPs are.
2. Create a USP for your business.
3. Share it with colleagues and ask their opinion. Ask if it makes sense. Ask if it is easy to understand. Ask if it captures the essence of your business.

WHAT DO YOU STAND FOR?

____

What is your USP?

____

THE PROFESSIONAL REFERENCE QUESTIONS LIST

How long have you known_________________?

How do you know______________________?

When was he/she hired?___________________

When did he/she leave? ___________________

What was his/her salary when he/she left?_________

Why did he/she leave?____________________

Did you work with him/her directly? ____________

Was he/she usually on time? ________________

Was he/she absent from work very often? _________

Did his/her personal life ever interfere with his/her work?

____

What were his/her titles? ___________________________

What were his/her duties? __________________________

Did he/she cooperate with supervisors? ________________

Did he/she cooperate with co-workers? ___________________

Did he/she take work home very often? ___________________

What are his/her primary attributes?______________________

What are his/her primary liabilities? _____________________

Is he/she eligible for rehire? ____________________________

Can you confirm the information he/she has given? _______

THE PERSONAL REFERENCE QUESTIONS LIST

How long have you known______________________?

How do you know____________________________?

What is your opinion of _________________________?

Does he/she get along well with others? ___________

Is he/she usually on time? ____________________________

Is he/she absent from work very often? _________

Does he/she bring work home very often? __________

Does he/she like his/her job? _________________________

What are his/her primary attributes?___________________

What are his/her primary liabilities? __________________

LEGAL VS ILLEGAL JOB INTERVIEW QUESTIONS HANDOUT

Note: this document is written from the perspective of an Employer

INQUIRY AREA

Illegal Questions

NATIONALITY ORIGIN/CITIZENSHIP

- Are you a Canadian/American citizen?
- Where were you/your parents born?
- What is your "native tongue"?
- Are you authorized to work in Canada?
- What language do you read/ speak/write fluently? (This question is okay only if this ability is relevant to the performance of the job.)

Age

- How old are you?
- When did you graduate?
- What's your birth date?
- Are you between the ages of 18 and 64?

Marital/Family Status

- What's your marital status?
- Whom do you live with?
- Do you plan to have a family? When?
- How many kids do you have?
- What are your child-care arrangements?
- Would you be willing to relocate if necessary?
- Would you be able and willing to travel as needed by the job? (This question is okay if it is asked of all applicants for the job.)
- Would you be able and willing to work overtime as necessary? (Again, this question is okay assuming it is asked of all applicants for the job.)

Affiliations

- What clubs or social organizations do you belong to?
- List any professional or trade groups or other organizations that you belong to that you consider relevant to your ability to perform this job.

Personal

- How tall are you? How much do you weigh? (Questions about height & weight are not acceptable unless minimum standards are essential to the safe performance of the job.)
- Are you able to lift a 30kg weight and carry it 100 metres/300 feet, as that is part of the job?

Disabilities

- Do you have any disabilities?
- Please complete the following medical history:
- Have you had any recent or past illnesses or operations? (If yes, list them and give dates when these occurred.)
- What was the date of your last physical exam?
- How's your family's health?
- When did you lose your eyesight? How?
- Do you need an accommodation to perform the job? (This question can only be asked after a job offer has been made.)
- Are you able to perform the essential functions of this job? (This question is okay if the interviewer has thoroughly described the job.)
- Can you demonstrate how you would perform the following job-related functions?
- As part of the hiring process, after a job offer has been made, you will be required to undergo a Medical exam. (Exam results must be kept strictly confidential, except medical/safety personnel may be informed if emergency medical treatment is required, and supervisors may be informed about necessary job accommodations, based on exam results.)

Arrest Record

- Have you ever been arrested?
- Have you ever been convicted of ________? (The crime named should be reasonably related to the performance of the job in question.)

Sex

- Are you male or female?

- What are the names & Relationships of persons living with you?
- You may be asked if you have ever worked under another name.

Race/Colour

- What is your race? What colour is your hair, eyes, or skin?
- No race-related questions are legal.

Religion

- What is your religious affiliation or denomination?
- What church do you belong to?
- What is the name of your pastor, minister, or rabbi?
- What religious holidays do you observe?
- None (If you wish to know if an applicant is available to work Saturday or Sunday shifts, ask: "Are you available to work on Saturdays and Sundays if needed?" Make sure you ask this question of all applicants.)

BEHAVIORAL/COMPETENCY BASED INTERVIEW QUESTIONS HANDOUT

Behavioral/Competency Based Interview Questions Handout

NOTE: AT THE END OF EACH EXAMPLE THERE IS A NOTATION OF WHAT competency the question is assessing.

1. Describe a situation in which you had to use reference materials to write a research paper. What was the topic? What journals did you read? (research/written communication)
2. Give me a specific example of a time when a co-worker or classmate criticized your work in front of others. How did you respond? How has that event shaped the way you communicate with others? (oral communication)
3. Give me a specific example of a time when you sold your supervisor or professor on an idea or concept. How did you proceed? What was the result? (assertiveness)
4. Describe the system you use for keeping track of multiple projects. How do you track your progress so that you can

meet deadlines? How do you stay focused? (commitment to task)

5. Tell me about a time when you came up with an innovative solution to a challenge your company or class was facing. What was the challenge? What role did others play? (creativity & imagination)
6. Describe a specific problem you solved for your employer or professor. How did you approach the problem? What role did others play? What was the outcome? (decision making)
7. Describe a time when you got co-workers or classmates who dislike each other to work together. How did you accomplish this? What was the outcome? (teamwork)
8. Tell me about a time when you failed to meet a deadline. What things did you fail to do? What were the repercussions? What did you learn? (time management)
9. Describe a time when you put your needs aside to help a co-worker or classmate understand a task. How did you assist them? What was the result? (flexibility)
10. Describe two specific goals you set for yourself and how successful you were in meeting them. What factors led to your success in meeting your goals?
11. Tell me about a time in which you had to use your written communication skills in order to get across an important point. (Decision Making)
12. Give me an example of a time you had to make a difficult decision. (Decision Making)
13. Describe a specific problem you solved for your employer. How did you approach the problem? What role did others play? What was the outcome?
14. Give me an example of when taking your time to make a decision paid off. (Initiative)
15. What did you do to prepare for this interview?
16. Give me an example of a situation that could not have happened successfully without you being there. (Planning & Organization)

17. Describe a situation when you had many projects due at the same time. What steps did you take to get them all done?
18. How do you determine priorities in scheduling your time? Give me an example. (Flexibility)
19. Describe a time where you were faced with problems or stresses that tested your coping skills.
20. Describe a time when you put your needs aside to help a co-worker understand a task. How did you assist them? What was the result? (Leadership)
21. Tell me about a time when you influenced the outcome of a project by taking a leadership role. (Leadership)
22. Give me an example of when you involved others in making a decision. (Time Management)
23. Tell me about a time when you failed to meet a deadline. What things did you fail to do? What were the repercussions? What did you learn?
24. Tell me about a time when you were particularly effective on prioritizing tasks and completing a project on schedule.

FOLLOW-UP IS EVERYTHING!

It can be a great feeling when coming home from a networking event and looking at the stack of business cards you have collected. You even spoke at length to many of the card-donators. Some, it can be a little difficult to recall who they actually were. "Now was he the tall fellow with the bad hair piece .... or was he?" You've probably experienced that scenario more than once. And you know what ... perhaps some of the business people that you gave your precious business card to are thinking something similar. Hopefully not about your bad hair though.

For effective business networking, I recommend the quality over quantity method of networking. Some would say that networking is a numbers game, the more that you meet the higher the chances of your meeting someone that can benefit you. Take for example that you are meeting someone for the first time and if the setting and conditions permit, they deliver their elevator pitch and you return with yours. Then comes the awkward moment, what to say next. You can either carry on conversing about something of no consequence "Nice day, eh?" until one of you tires of it or you can explore common interests. Assuming that you have a common interest, I would suggest that you take the lead in the conversation in getting the other to expand upon the commonality or something that they had previously said.

Many networkers make the mistake of trying to sell their product or themselves at this juncture. Your goal should be to arrange to meet them at another time, perhaps for coffee, to discuss those common areas further. Even though many of us are electronically connected to our offices by our smart phones and can likely check to see if we are available at a certain date and time to make a coffee date, we likely won't. When you suggest meeting for coffee, later, if the person is willing to set up a date and time, on the spot, I would go with it. Location can always be determined later by e-mail.

If they aren't willing to set a time and date, I would refer to their business card and say something to the effect of "Can I reach you at this e-mail? I'll contact you next week and see if we can set up a time to get together for a quick coffee." Unfortunately, for many networkers, this is as far as they go. They don't do the follow-up. Life gets busy, there is always one more thing to do with your business and before you know it you have lost the window of opportunity. There is a strong possibility that the individual that you were networking with also has a list of people they are following up with and other commitments. It is far too easy to get left by the wayside if you don't take action to stand out from the others.

At a recent morning meeting of a business networking group we discussed the issue of follow up. One of our members related that in his experience, if you actually follow-up with a lead, it puts you way ahead of those that don't. He makes a practice of following up with a networking connection within three days of the original meeting and says that it is amazing how many people have said "You know, you are one of the few that actually follows up." Yes, following up can help you stand out from the competition.

The coffee get together is the opportunity for each of you to share your business details and determine if there is enough reason to continue at another time to develop your relationship further and ideally to do business together.

You might ask "I've contacted them three times by e-mail and even left a couple voice mails but they haven't gotten back to me. What do I do next?" There could be a legitimate reason for them not getting back to you. Life happens! But they could be acting non-assertively and are actively avoiding you. I would have to respond with "If that was true, is that someone that you really want to network with or to do business with?" If you are to continue it could easily label you as a stalker.

One suggestion may be to add them to your tickler file. A couple weeks down the road, ignoring the fact that they haven't acknowledged you yet, you would be justified in sending them a message something like "I just noticed that we didn't get together a few weeks ago like we said we would. Where did the time go? It seems to be picking up speed. Last time we met we were discussing our common interests of ...Are you still interested in getting together?" If you still don't receive a response, I would put them in the "inactive" file.

When it comes to networking, to stand out from your competition, remember to follow-up.

ABOUT THE AUTHOR

Rae A. Stonehouse is a Canadian born author & speaker.

His professional career as a Registered Nurse working predominantly in psychiatry/mental health, has spanned four decades.

Rae has embraced the principal of CANI (Constant and Never-ending Improvement) as promoted by thought leaders such as Tony Robbins and brings that philosophy to each of his publications and presentations.

Rae has dedicated the latter segment of his journey through life to overcoming his personal inhibitions. As a 25+ year member of Toastmasters International he has systematically built his self-confidence and communicating ability. He is passionate about sharing his lessons with his readers and listeners.

His publications thus far are of the self-help, self-improvement genre and systematically offer valuable sage advice on a specific topic.

His writing style can be described as being conversational. As an author, Rae strives to have a one-to-one conversation with each of his readers, very much like having your own personal self-development coach.

Rae is known for having a wry sense of humour that features in his publications. To learn more about Rae A. Stonehouse, visit the Wonderful World of Rae Stonehouse at http://raestonehouse.com.

1. PUBLICATIONS BY THE AUTHOR

Publications by the Author:

POWER NETWORKING FOR SHY PEOPLE: TIPS & TECHNIQUES FOR Moving from Shy to Sly! http://powernetworkingforshypeople.com

~

PROtect Yourself! Empowering Tips & Techniques for Personal Safety: A Practical Violence Prevention Manual for Healthcare Workers http://protectyourselfnow.ca/

~

E=Emcee Squared: Tips & Techniques to Becoming a Dynamic Master of Ceremonies http://emceesquared.mremcee.com/

~

Power of Promotion: On-line Marketing for Toastmasters Club Growth http://powerofpromotion.ca/

~

You're Hired! Job Search Strategies That Work (This is the complete program)

E-book & Paperback: https://books2read.com/yourehired

On-line E-course: http://liveforexcellenceacademy.com/

(Available as a self-directed or instructor-led program)

~

You're Hired! Resume Tactics: Job Search Strategies That Work

E-book & Paperback: https://books2read.com/resumetactics

On-line E-course: http://liveforexcellenceacademy.com/

~

Job Interview Preparation: Job Search Strategies That Work

E-book& Paperback: books2read.com/jobinterviewpreparation

On-line E-course: http://liveforexcellenceacademy.com/

~

You're Hired! Leveraging Your Network: Job Search Strategies That Work

E-book & Paperback: http://books2read.com/leveragingyournetwork

On-line E-course: http://liveforexcellenceacademy.com/

YOU'RE HIRED! POWER TACTICS: JOB SEARCH STRATEGIES THAT WORK (This is a box set containing the complete content of Resume Tactics, Job Interview Preparation & Leveraging Your Network)

E-book: http://books2read.com/powertactics

IF YOU HAVE FOUND THIS BOOK AND PROGRAM TO BE HELPFUL, PLEASE leave us a warm review on Amazon.com

www.ingramcontent.com/pod-product-compliance
Lightning Source LLC
Chambersburg PA
CBHW071321210326
41597CB00015B/1299

* 9 7 8 1 9 9 9 4 7 5 4 0 6 *